UNDERSTANDING

EQUINE
NUTRITION

REVISED EDITION

UNDERSTANDING

EQUINE NUTRITION

Your guide to horse health care and management

REVISED EDITION

BY KAREN BRIGGS

the HORSE HEALTH CARE LIBRARY

ECLIPSE PRESS

Lexington, Kentucky

Library of Congress Control Number: 2006935786

ISBN 978-1-58150-155-1

Printed in the United States
First Edition: 1998
Revised Edition: 2007

Contents

Introduction

Mother Nature didn't mean for it to be so complicated. Feeding the horse, one of her most elegant creations, was supposed to be a simple thing. He and his associated equines (donkeys, asses, zebras, and a few other extinct varieties) had evolved to roam the grasslands of the world, deriving all of their nutritional needs from the tough, fibrous grasses and weeds they found there. Superbly adapted to break up stemmy plants with his large, sideways-grinding jaws and flat molars, and equipped with a digestive system ideally designed for the slow, fermentative digestion of fiber, the horse was pretty much set — all he needed was some fair-to-poor pastureland, a source of fresh water, and a natural salt lick he probably shared with many other creatures.

Left to his own devices, he wandered and grazed for 12 to 20 hours per day, those jaws methodically doing their job while his prehensile lips searched for the choicest shoots and leaves.

In the last few thousand years, the horse has found himself living a life quite different from that for which he was originally designed. Having been domesticated for work or for pleasure, he no longer was free to travel the grasslands and pick and choose his meals. Instead, he was more than likely housed in a box or standing stall for the convenience of his keepers, and fed at intervals that suited his masters more than his digestive tract.

Being a stabled horse did have its perks, however. In the winter, instead of risking starvation when heavy snows might cover all the grazing, there was hay — dried grasses stored for just such an occasion. And there was also grain, which was offered to give the horse more energy for the work he did, and which was, frankly, delicious.

But to this day, the changes we have made to the horse's natural diet are not always in his best interest. Restricted exercise and rigid feeding schedules were never in Nature's plan for the horse. Nor was the consumption of concentrated carbohydrates. All three can be the cause of considerable digestive upset for the horse, who has not yet managed to adapt his gastrointestinal tract to our requirements.

His surprisingly small stomach (only about twice the size of a domestic pig's) is ill-equipped to handle large quantities of feed in a small time frame, and the lack of a reverse peristalsis reflex means he can neither vomit nor burp, an evolutionary oversight that puts him at risk when the stomach is overloaded. Add to that the troubles involved with digesting concentrated, energy-rich feedstuff he was never designed to eat, and it starts to become obvious why feed-related woes like colic, developmental orthopedic disease, laminitis, gastric ulcers, and dental difficulties are so common — and so dangerous.

Somewhere along the way, feeding horses got complicated. Fear not — it can be made simple again. That's what *Understanding Equine Nutrition* is about — making sense of the jargon, sorting out the ingredients, and making a plan and a menu that supply all the nutrients your horse needs. Whether you have a growing yearling, a high-performance athlete, a weekend pleasure mount, a brood-mom-to-be, or a dearly loved retiree, there are common-sense solutions that also will get you the best value for your feed dollar. Not to mention some peace of mind. For while we can't always duplicate Mother Nature's plan for the horse, we can certainly come up with some very viable alternatives.

What Does A Horse Need?

I t's often been observed that horses are simple creatures. And while the phrase might have been unkindly intended to describe a lack of intellectual complexity, it's pretty accurate when it comes to their nutritional needs.

Unlike us humans with our omnivorous tastes, horses are strictly plant eaters. Forage is the basis of the equine diet, and when the forage is of good quality and in plentiful supply, horses suffer few digestive difficulties. It's only when we deviate from the "forage principle" that our horses run into trouble.

At first glance, however, the equine digestive tract seems to be something of an evolutionary mistake. Take the equine stomach, for example. It's surprisingly small for an animal the size of the horse — with a capacity of only about two to four gallons (or 7.5 to 15 liters). In contrast, the small intestine can measure an amazing 70 feet (about 22 meters) in length, if uncoiled and stretched out, with a diameter of three to four inches and a capacity for 10 to 12 gallons of material. Compared with what we know about the physiology of other animals, the horse's equine gastrointestinal tract seems strangely out of proportion. But from Nature's point of view, everything's just fine. In his wild state, the horse never expected to ingest large quantities of food at one sitting; his digestive system is optimally designed for his wandering, grazing lifestyle.

Let's take a slightly more thorough tour through the equine innards and see what else we can discover about the link between his physiology and his diet.

When a horse tears off a mouthful of grass with his teeth or uses his talented lips to pick up hay or grain from the ground or a feed tub, the tongue transfers the food to the back of his mouth. There, the horse's wide, flat molars grind it up and mix it with saliva (which almost immediately launches the digestive process by beginning to break down starches). When thoroughly chewed, a mouthful of oats will have absorbed its own weight in moisture while a mouthful of hay will have absorbed about four times its own weight.

From there, the base of the tongue pushes the food past the soft palate and into the pharynx, the opening to the esophagus, a flexible tube that leads down the neck to the stomach. Once in the esophagus, a series of muscular contractions pushes the food along. In the case of the horse, these contractions move only one direction — meaning that what goes down, for better or worse, stays down.

Surprisingly little digestion goes on in the stomach itself. A small microbial population initiates some fermentation, and there is also some enzymatic action — but because food remains in the stomach only 15 minutes, on average, before being pushed on to the small intestine, there is little time for any major food breakdown. As soon as the stomach reaches about two-thirds of its capacity, it typically starts to pass food (which, by now, has been liquefied by the stomach acids) on to the small intestine, and the process continues as long as the horse keeps eating.

Although food remains in the stomach for a very brief interval, its presence (or absence) has a direct bearing on the horse's health. The upper, inner portion of the stomach's lining is made up of a non-glandular, squamous cell layer that is vulnerable to the hydrochloric acid the stomach secretes. Having food in the stomach at frequent intervals tends to absorb the acid and keep it from splashing this upper layer. Horses fed infrequently (one or two large meals a day, rather than several smaller meals) are more at risk of gastric ulcers, which can result from exposure to stomach acids. And it's worth noting, too, that forage does the best job of absorbing these acids. Horses fed a hay-only diet typically have a very low incidence of ulcers while those on a mixed diet are more at risk.

The next stop on the tour is the small intestine, a coiled and convoluted tube suspended from the loin region by a fan-shaped membrane called the mesentery. The first section of the small intestine, the duodenum, is shaped like a U-turn, which helps prevent food from being forced back into the stomach if the small intestine becomes distended. The small intestine is the primary site for protein digestion and the absorption of amino acids (although grains are processed more thoroughly here than is forage), and it can hold up to 30% of the GI tract's total capacity.

Inside the small intestine, enzymes go to work to break down food materials. Starch not already digested by saliva is converted to a simple sugar called maltose, and other complex sugars and carbohydrates are broken down to simple-sugar forms so they can be absorbed through the intestinal walls. (Capillaries transport them into the blood, and they eventually arrive at the liver, the horse's major chemical processing plant. The liver also sorts amino acids and reorganizes them into proteins and binds water-soluble nutrients to their appropriate carriers for distribution throughout the body.)

The small intestine is also the primary site for the digestion and absorption of fats. Most animals use gallbladder secretions to break down fats, but horses have no gallbladder, another little evolutionary peculiarity. Nonetheless, horses seem able to use diets containing 10% to 15% fat very efficiently for energy and weight gain. (More on fats in chapter 6.) Finally, the fat-soluble vitamins A, D, E, and K are absorbed in the small intestine, as are calcium, some phosphorus, and B vitamins.

On average, it takes 60 to 90 minutes for food, now liquefied, to pass through the length of the small intestine.

The last portion of the small intestine, the ileum, leads to the final section of the gastrointestinal tour, the hindgut, made up of the cecum, large (or ascending) colon, small colon, rectum, and anus. Here's where the bulk of digestion's hard work is done. And instead of enzymes doing the honors, digestion in the hindgut is largely microbial — performed by a population of billions of symbiotic bacteria that efficiently break down plant fibers into simpler compounds called volatile fatty acids (VFAs), which can be absorbed through the gut wall. Not only are these bacteria a natural part of the digestive process, they're essential to it — as we'll see later when we discuss fiber digestion in more detail.

The cecum, approximately four feet long and with a capacity of seven to nine gallons, is a huge factory for the first stage of hindgut digestion. The cecum originates high in the horse's right flank area and extends down and forward toward the diaphragm. Plant fibers, composed of cellulose and other hard-to-digest molecules, pass through the stomach and small intestine unaffected by enzymes, but when they hit the "fermentation vat of the cecum," the population of bacteria there makes short work of them, usually breaking them down in about five hours. The size and structure of the cecum (the physiological equivalent to our appendix, but far more useful) are such that it slows the passage of food in order for the microbes to do their job.

From the cecum, the partially digested food moves to the large colon, where fermentation continues. Almost 12 feet in length, on average, and holding an impressive volume of 14 to 16 gallons, or 50 to 60 liters, of food (about 38% of the GI tract's total capacity), the large colon is also where food dwells longest — between 36 and 48 hours. It has a sacculated construction that resembles a series of pouches. This not only can facilitate the breakdown of large quantities of fibrous material but also can become a risk factor when the pouches become distended with gas during a bout of colic, as they seem custom-made for twisting and even strangulating their own tissues.

Once the food has been thoroughly processed in the large colon, it moves to the small colon, another 10 to 12 feet long but smaller in diameter (about four inches). The vast majority of the nutrients have been absorbed by this time, and what's left in the gut is whatever the horse cannot digest or use. The main function of this portion of the hindgut is to reclaim excess moisture from the remaining material. By the time the food leaves the small colon, it has become solid again and has been molded into fecal balls. The small colon empties into the rectum, and some 36 to 72 hours after beginning its journey, the waste material from a horse's meal is expelled as manure through the anus.

The equine gastrointestinal tract functions very well under normal conditions. But as every horseman knows, it's also extremely sensitive and easy to upset. Any sudden change in diet, for example, can severely compromise the population of gut bacteria so essential for fiber digestion — and when these bacteria start dying off, the horse is at risk of colic or, at the very least, of not getting all the nutrients out of his feed. That's why it's always best to make feed changes over a couple of weeks rather than suddenly.

Another trigger for digestive upset occurs when the horse receives a large, carbohydrate-rich meal (typically, one that is light on forage and heavy on grain). Under these conditions, the small intestine might not be able to process and absorb completely all of the nutrients before the meal moves on to the hindgut. When excess amounts of soluble carbohydrates reach the fermentation vat of the cecum, they are processed to produce not only VFAs but also lactic acid. An increase in lactic acid lowers the overall hindgut pH level, which in turn can make the environment hostile for the gut bacteria. Bacteria begin to die off, and in the process can release endotoxins (poisons). Between these endotoxins and the lactic acid itself, the stage might be set for colic or laminitis. Suddenly the old horseman's rule of feeding small amounts often begins to make a lot of sense, particularly if your horse is on a high-grain diet.

So, what do horses actually *need* in their diets? The basics are fresh, clean water; access to salt; and forage — lots of it. As a general rule of thumb, horses should consume between 1.5% and 3% of their own body weight in feed every day — and at least half of that (and often much more) should be forage of some kind. Whether it's pasture, hay, or some other form of roughage isn't as important as the quantity because the horse's gut literally needs that amount to stay in good digestive health.

Is grain necessary? Often, the answer is no. Remember that in the wild, horses have no access to concentrated forms of carbohydrates and little need for them because they are not doing "work" in the sense that we humans demand. When we domesticated the horse, we asked him to expend energy over and above what he would normally do in the course of his wild day; grains help provide the fuel he needs to perform for us. In addition, we bred horses to be larger, stronger, faster, more elegant — and, often, less hardy and more dependent on high-energy concentrates to maintain a healthy body weight. Nonetheless, grain always should be considered an optional add-on to the diet. It should be fed as necessary only to supplement the nutrition provided by the horse's forage and in accordance with his condition, his metabolism, and the amount of work expected of him.

In the chapters to follow, we'll explore each of the ingredients of the equine diet in more detail. And we'll get a firmer grasp on how to combine those ingredients to make a healthy daily ration that provides all the essential nutrients and makes good economic sense.

The Hydrated Horse

Any treatise on caring for horses you've ever read probably includes the line, "Provide access to plenty of fresh, clean water." Though we all understand that this is good advice — after all, all living things need this simple, essential liquid — we don't tend to give water a lot of consideration as part of the equine diet.

The reality is that water is the most important nutrient, bar none. Without water almost all of your horse's systems cease to function. Here are just a few ways in which water is essential:

• aids in thermoregulation (the maintenance of the horse's body temperature)

• lubricates the joints

• helps cushion the central nervous system

• is involved in both sight and hearing

• aids in digestion

• acts as a solvent for toxins and helps eliminate them through urine and sweat

• and helps maintain an elastic skin tone.

To give you another perspective on water's importance, consider that horses can survive without food for up to three weeks — but they can only survive without water for a maximum of five to six days. Though water intake varies according to the horse's exertion level, the ambient temperature, the components of his diet, and other factors, the average 1,000-pound horse needs a bare minimum of three to eight gallons a day to function at a maintenance level.

Horses quickly become dehydrated without sufficient water. Within 24 hours of water deprivation, they may lose about 4% of their bodyweight, through a combination of sweating and urination, manure, and respiration. After 48 hours without water, they have lost 6.8% of their body-

AT A GLANCE

◆ Water is a horse's most important nutrient.

◆ Horses quickly become dehydrated without sufficient water.

◆ Insufficient water, especially during winter months, can quickly lead to colic.

◆ It's a good idea to test water annually for contaminants.

weight; after 72 hours, about 9% ... and if summer heat is involved, that number may skyrocket to 16%. The symptoms of dehydration — dry mucous membranes, sunken eyes, a tucked-up appearance, skin that has lost its elasticity, and a slowed capillary refill time — only become obvious when the horse already has lost 6% of his bodyweight or more. By that time, dehydration has already wreaked its devastating effect on athletic performance and digestive efficiency. Both functions take a nosedive in the absence of water — and decreased digestive function can quickly lead to colic (see chapter 12). In fact, the main reason the incidence of colic increases from December to March is that many horses don't drink enough water in the winter months (often because their water supply has been allowed to freeze over).

Winter isn't the only time horses are at risk for colic due to restricted water intake, however. Any time a horse faces a rapid decrease in water consumption, he'll be more prone to impaction colic, especially if a good part of his diet is dried forage. Horses grazing fresh, juicy spring pasture can extract most of their water needs from their grass intake, but those eating hay or roughage cubes need to drink significantly more so that their gastrointestinal systems can churn the dried forage into a digestible slurry.

Mares in foal or lactating (or both) have increased needs for water, largely because they are satisfying their increased energy and protein needs by taking in more feed but also because they lose some

Horses need ready access to water to prevent dehydration.

water in the placental fluids and in producing milk. Although foals satisfy most of their liquid requirements by nursing, most will begin to drink water at the age of only one to two weeks. It's a habit that begins early and lasts a lifetime.

The other reason horses become dehydrated is excessive water loss through sweating, as can happen in heat and humidity, especially when stressful exercise is involved. When temperatures are high, water needs can increase by three to four times with work.

Horses with diarrhea or scours also become dehydrated quite rapidly, and the water loss in this case makes thermoregulation difficult and contributes to fever.

Whatever the reason behind it, dehydration is a situation best prevented. The easiest way to ensure your horse never gets dehydrated is to make sure he always has access to clean, fresh water, regardless of the weather.

Straight From the Source

Making clean water available sounds like a very basic thing, but it's not always as simple as it sounds. Water completely untouched by chemicals or minerals doesn't exist in nature. Water is, after all, the universal solvent, with a unique ability to pick up and dissolve virtually everything it encounters. These other substances contained in drinking water aren't necessarily bad; minerals dissolved in water impart much of its flavor, after all, and many are even beneficial (such as fluoride in city water supplies). The issue with dissolved substances isn't so much purity as it is safety — in other words, it's not whether they are present, but whether they are present in toxic amounts.

If you live in suburbia, your barn may draw its water from a public or municipal system that provides extensive purification and filtration services and also regularly tests its water for contaminants such as disease-causing bacteria, toxic chemicals, and even radioactive elements such as radon. Worries are few with this sort of system, but that doesn't mean there's no possibility of contamination; the testing is done at the source, and if there is damage to the delivery line or a problem with the plumbing on your property, your water could still be compromised.

More diligence is required if, like the majority of horse people, you draw your barn's water from a well. Many wells provide beautifully clean water, but there is also the potential for contamination. The same is true if your horse gets his water from a natural source, such as a stream or pond in your pasture. Fortunately, horses are well adapted to dealing with less-than-pristine water sources.

Like us, however, their water intake can quickly be adversely affected if the water's taste is unpleasant. Horses that refuse to drink from unfamiliar-tasting water sources are distressingly common (so much so that most of us are familiar with the trick of flavoring water with anything from peppermint oil to powdered kids' drinks to disguise the taste when these finicky horses are away from home).

The single most reliable indicator of water quality in your barn is the total amount of dissolved solids (TDS), a number that can easily be determined with a water test run by your county or state health laboratory, your local agricultural extension agent, or the Environmental Protection Agency. TDS is the sum of the concentrations of all organic and inorganic substances dissolved in the water, including mineral salts, algae, bacteria, nitrates, and solid particles of debris. Between 1,000 and 2,999 parts per million TDS is considered satisfactory for livestock, with 6,500 ppm the usual upper limit for safe drinking water for horses. At levels above 1,000 ppm, your water may have an offensive smell, taste, or color — and a 1998 study conducted by the Equine Research Centre in Guelph, Ontario, found that equine diarrhea is a common complaint on farms with water TDS levels in excess of 1,000.

Testing your well's water for bacterial contamination on an annual basis is sound practice. A total coliform test checks the water for bacteria normally found in the soil, in surface water, and in human and animal waste. Coliform bacteria are not, in themselves, considered harmful, but their presence in your water supply is an indication that your well may be contaminated either from run-off from a manure pile, from a nearby septic bed or tank, or from fertilizer or manure spread on a nearby farmer's field. Coliform levels can rise in drought conditions, with sudden heavy rainfalls, or with any unusual change in weather patterns. It's also possible to have high coliform levels when the well has developed physical defects, such as a broken or missing cap that could allow debris, surface water, insects, or rodents inside.

Doing bacterial testing is a good idea whenever there is a noticeable change in the color, odor, or taste of your water; when any animal or person on your farm becomes sick from a water-borne disease such as Potomac Horse Fever or *Salmonella*; when the water supply system on your farm has been disassembled for repairs; when spring flooding occurs near your well; or when the cap or the interior of the well has been damaged.

Wells that are correctly drilled, sealed, and more than 50 feet deep generally have less chance of becoming contaminated with bacteria. Water from an old or shallow well should be tested more frequently. Don't rely on "clean" tests from a neighbor's well. Even two wells side by side can draw water from separate aquifers (underground water sources) and yield very different results.

Other Contaminants

Well water often contains significant concentrations of dissolved minerals that can influence the taste, smell, and palatability of your water. (The classic example is "sulfur water," which has that unmistakable rotten-egg stench.) Your local lab can test your water for levels of calcium, magnesium, manganese, iron, copper, zinc, sodium, chloride, and lead, as well as sulfates and nitrates (nitrate contamination is particularly common on horse farms; its likely source, your manure pile). Concentrations of these minerals, if sufficiently high, can also have an impact on your horse's dietary balance, as levels of one mineral in his gut can often influence his ability to absorb another.

Some minerals, such as iron, calcium, and magnesium, are chiefly a concern because they can clog your plumbing with scale and deposits and change the water's color and taste. Other minerals, such as lead, are more worrisome because they can build up to toxic levels. (See chapter 8 for more on minerals.)

An acidity/alkalinity test is another frequently performed water analysis. Water testing below pH 6.5 is considered acidic and can contribute to the corrosion of your pipes. (Acidic water isn't necessarily as nasty as it sounds, however — a can of carbonated soda may be up to 100 times more acidic than water with a pH of 5.0.) On the other hand, if your water tests at pH 8.5 or higher, it has a lot of alkaline, which means you probably have crusty mineral deposits on your pipes and fixtures. A sudden change in your water's pH can be a heads up for damage to your well as the pH levels in water usually fluctuate very little over time.)

Blue-green algae occasionally bloom in ponds in hot, dry weather and can be a concern if your chief water source is above ground. Blue-green algae poisoning can cause muscle tremors, labored breathing, bloody diarrhea, liver damage, and even convulsions and death — so it's best to remove horses from a contaminated water source with algal blooms immediately. Algal growth is usually associated with large amounts of organic material in the water, often as a result of runoff from nearby fertilized fields.

When it comes to water safety, pesticides and herbicides are other worries. Though expensive, testing for these chemicals may be worth doing if you have significant concerns about the agricultural sprays being used in your area. Likewise, if you suspect solvents or other toxic chemicals may have leached into your water supply from a local industrial site, get your water tested for your own peace of mind.

Guidelines for Testing

• If your water has an unpleasant smell or your horses refuse to drink it, test for the following: pH, copper, lead, iron, zinc, sodium, chloride, TDS, and hydrogen sulfide.

• If your water is cloudy and frothy, test for turbidity (cloudiness, caused by mud, algae, and solids), TDS, and detergents.

• If you live near a road salt storage site, a street that is heavily salted in winter, or the ocean, test for sodium and chloride levels.

What should you do if your water tests reveal an imbalance or contamination? Consult the lab that did your testing for its recommendations, and try these tactics:

• Improve the protection for your well, giving it a weatherproof, sanitary seal and eliminating access for debris, insects, and rodents

• Eliminate the source of the contamination (i.e., remove or relocate the manure pile);

• Treat the water with chemicals or filtration to improve its quality, if that's what your lab recommends.

When all else fails, you may have to drill a new well. Newer, deeper wells with good seals are far less problematic than older, shallower wells that may be chronically contaminated. Though the cost of a new well can be considerable, it will benefit you and your horses in the long run.

Manure Pile Management

If high coliform levels turn up in your well water, it's possible your own manure management is to blame. To protect your groundwater, make sure you situate your manure pile in an elevated, well-drained location, not on the lowest spot on the property. After a rainstorm, watch the flow of water — it should go around your manure pile, not through it. Simply rerouting the flow of run-off water can improve your water quality considerably. Make sure, too, that the natural run-off from your manure pile doesn't head directly toward any ponds or streams. Finally, don't park your manure pile in a paddock where your horses can climb over and through it all day. They'll pack it and spread it over a greater area, increasing the probability of water contamination.

Protein

O f all the components of your horse's diet, protein is probably the most misunderstood. Long assumed to function as an energy source for the body, protein mainly functions to provide amino acids (the building blocks of bones, muscles, and soft tissues) for growth and repair.

What are amino acids good for? Virtually all of the horse's vital processes, it seems. Amino acids are involved in the synthesis and the release of hormones, the synthesis of neurotransmitters and enzymes, and the regulation of sleep, appetite, and blood pressure, to name just a few functions. But primarily, amino acids are needed for the formation and repair of muscle tissue and other soft tissues throughout the body. On a fat-free, moisture-free basis, they account for approximately 80% of a horse's total structure.

Growing horses, which are 'building' new tissues as they mature, and horses used for breeding, have higher protein requirements than do mature horses being used for pleasure or performance. Whether working or idle, most mature horses need surprisingly small amounts of protein.

Inside a Protein Molecule

Proteins are "chains" made up of various combinations of the twenty-two different amino acids that exist in nature. Amino acids are relatively simple organic compounds, consisting of a basic amino group and an acidic carboxyl group. Carbohydrates and fats also contain carbon atoms with hydrogen and oxygen atoms attached, but amino acids alone contain nitrogen and sometimes sulfur. The position and number of the amino acids in a single protein make up its "amino acid profile."

When a horse ingests protein, enzymes and acids break up the chain of amino acids in the digestive tract, and the individual amino acids are absorbed through the wall of the small intestine and into the bloodstream via the liver. From there, they travel to the sites where they are most needed for growth or repair of tissues.

Although amino acids are absorbed from the small intestine in a format relatively unchanged from their original chemical composition, the horse's body does have the ability to change some amino acids into different formats as the need exists, a process that occurs in the liver. However, the body does not have the ability to create all the amino acids it needs. Some amino acids can only be synthesized by micro-organisms or green plants. These are called the "essential" amino acids, and the horse must obtain them from his environment. ("Non-essential" amino acids are those the horse can synthesize himself.)

A good quality protein source is a food that provides a sufficient amount of these essential amino acids, particularly the amino acids lysine and methionine. Lysine is often called the "first limiting" amino acid — meaning that if insufficient quantities of lysine are present, then the horse's body will have difficulty using any of the other amino acids available. Methionine is second in importance.

The amino acid profile of a feed is more important for a young, growing horse than for a mature one; adult horses are far less sensitive to differences in protein quality. Nor does it matter to the horse whether a particular amino acid comes from a natural source or whether it is chemically synthesized. Lysine and methionine are often deficient in horse feeds, and as they can be synthesized inexpensively, it's quite routine for feed companies to add these ingredients to improve the overall amino acid profile biochemically. (Not all amino acids can be easily synthesized, however.)

Can protein serve as an energy source? Well, yes, but metabolically it's an expensive process, producing three to six times more heat than the breakdown of carbohydrates or fats and yielding considerably less energy. The heating factor might be beneficial in a cold environment, but it also might contribute to excessive sweating and possible heat exhaustion during hard work, especially in a warmer climate. And because protein is one of the more expensive ingredients in a feed, it's impractical to feed higher levels of protein in search of a performance advantage. You'll do far better by upping the levels of carbohydrates and fats — which we'll talk about in chapters four and five.

Assessing Protein Levels

Most of us determine a feed's protein level by looking at the percentage value on the feed tag under "crude protein." But the crude protein numbers can be deceptive. They do not really reflect either the overall quality of the protein (which can only be determined by the amino acid profile), or the amount of protein from that feed that the horse can digest and use. The crude protein (CP) value is based on the overall nitrogen content of a feed, and not all of the nitrogen in a feed sample is necessarily protein-bound. Nitrogen also can be found in purines, creatinine, ammonium salts, and nucleic acids, all of which might be in a feed sample. In cattle feeds, a common non-protein source of nitrogen is urea, which is added to help cattle synthesize their own proteins when the nitrogen is made available in their guts. Urea also can be found in some horse feeds, but horses are not equipped to use it the way cattle are. It does no harm but also has no benefit.

Feed companies calculate the crude protein value of a feed based on a chemical analysis of the overall nitrogen content of a feed. Based on the idea that most proteins contain about 16% nitrogen, plus or minus 2%, the nitrogen content of a feed is divided by 0.16 (or multiplied by 6.25 for the same result) to arrive at the crude protein value. For example, if you know a feed has a nitrogen content of 1.6%, the crude protein of that product would be 10%.

The possibility of non-protein-bound nitrogen sources in the feed makes the CP level, at best, an estimate of what the horse actually can digest and use. As a rule, you can estimate that most grain products are somewhere between 2% to 5% lower in digestible protein (DP) than the CP numbers indicate. A product described as being 14% crude protein probably would deliver 9% to 12% DP. The difference is more dramatic with hay. Depending on the stage of bloom in which the hay was cut, sometimes only about 50% of the protein might be digestible.

The availability of amino acids in a grain ration can be adversely affected by denaturing or oxidation as a result of long storage (particularly in warm conditions or bright sunlight) or improper heating (as can sometimes occur during a pelleting or extruding process). Inadequate drying of a heated feed, prior to storage, also can reduce the protein digestibility. Some feed companies anticipate these problems with feeds that undergo heat processing, and add supplemental levels of lysine (and sometimes other amino acids as well) to compensate.

Excesses and Deficiencies

Horses that receive inadequate amounts of protein in their diets can suffer a number of ill effects, including decreased growth and development in youngsters, and reduced appetite, body tissue weight loss, slow hoof growth, energy deficit, and a poor hair coat with reduced shedding in adults. Pregnant mares with protein deficiencies may become more prone to abortions, and lactating mares suffer declines in milk production. Muscle deterioration, especially in the large muscle groups of the hindquarters, also might be evident, and some horses will begin eating manure. The reduced food intake of a depressed, protein-deficient horse can become a vicious cycle, making efforts to correct the condition difficult. But the protein requirements of an adult horse are low enough that true protein deficiencies are quite rare. They usually occur only when a horse is on very poor pasture or hay with no other supplemental feed, for a prolonged period of time. With a corrected diet, most of the signs of protein deficiency in adult horses can be turned around in as little as a week. The damage done to a young, growing horse, however, can be more serious.

Poor pasture can contribute to protein deficiency, although the condition is uncommon.

More common, and equally damaging, is an excess of protein in the diet, especially in mature horses that have been fed by owners laboring under the misunderstanding that protein equals energy. Here's what happens: Protein not used immediately by the horse's system is broken down to release the nitrogen atoms (the rest of the molecule being stored), and those nitrogen atoms become bound up as ammonia and urea molecules. The ammonia and urea eventually are excreted in the urine, which leads to increased water intake, increased urination, and a noticeably strong ammonia smell in the stall. And before ammonia and urea can be excreted in the urine, they must be filtered out of the blood — a process that, over time, can tax the kidneys. It's conceivable that this eventually might lead to decreased renal function, and that then the unfiltered urea and ammonia in the bloodstream can exacerbate liver and kidney disease.

Decreased athletic performance is another possible outcome of a high-protein diet. Lower blood pH at rest, and during sprinting exercise, has recently been demonstrated in horses fed abnormally high levels of protein And In addition to all this, there's some evidence that excess protein can interfere with calcium absorption the absorption of both calcium and phosphorus. Researchers differ, however, on how much damage a high-protein diet can cause, and how long a horse must be fed such a diet before the effects (if any) are noticeable. There is stronger evidence for the detrimental effect of excess protein in growing horses — in one study, weanlings and yearlings fed a diet 25% higher in protein than normal suffered slower rates of growth overall and higher incidences of developmental bone and joint problems.

How Much Is Enough?

So what is an appropriate level of protein for your horse? Continuing research is changing that answer all the time, but there are some general guidelines. The amount of crude protein needed in the diet depends on the needs of the individual horse (the most pivotal question being, is he still growing?), the digestibility or "bioavailability" of the protein, and the amount of the diet consumed. As a rule, though, a value of 0.60 g of digestible protein (1.26 g of crude protein) per kilogram of body weight per day is appropriate for most adult horses for maintenance metabolism.

Broodmares in their first eight months of gestation trimester of pregnancy don't really need supplemental levels of protein, but in their last trimester, when the fetus does 60% to 65% of its growing, from the fifth month on, their protein requirements increase. Lactation (nursing) also demands higher protein levels; the protein content of mare's milk is highest right after foaling and decreases gradually as the lactation period progresses. In one study, nursing broodmares fed less than 2.8 g of crude protein per kilogram of bodyweight per day lost weight and produced less milk than mares fed at least 3.2 g of crude protein per kilo of bodyweight per day. Protein deficiencies in the mare's diet also have an adverse effect on the growth of the nursing foal.

After three months of nursing, most mares are producing fairly small amounts of milk — and foals are starting to eat more solid food. At this point, a return to regular protein levels is appropriate for most mares.

Some researchers feel that during the breeding season, stallions also can benefit from a higher level of dietary protein, which is scaled back once breeding is finished for the year.

And hard exercise (such as racing, three-day eventing, or endurance racing) does increase the need for protein in the diet of adult horses, to support increased muscle development and mass, and to replace nitrogen lost in sweat. But the overall increase is quite small — just 1% to 2%.

Which feeds provide the best protein? Interestingly, animal sources, such as milk and egg protein, and even fish and meat meal, offer the best amino acid profile and the highest levels of lysine. Milk protein is often used as the primary protein source for foal feeds, but because it is quite expensive (and because adult horses are far less sensitive to protein quality differences), it's rarely found in feeds for mature animals.

Among the plant sources, soybean and canola meal are the next best things — they are the only two plant protein products that contain adequate amounts of lysine and methionine. Other common protein sources, such as linseed meal and cottonseed meal, have poor amino acid profiles and are generally supplemented with amino acids added by the feed manufacturer. Grains themselves (such as oats, corn, and barley) can contain between 8% and 20% protein, but it's of poor quality — which is the reason most feed companies add a higher-quality protein supplement to their "balanced" feeds (sweetfeeds, pellets, and other pre-mixed rations). If the manufacturers have done their job, the feed should contain at least 0.65% lysine (on a dry matter basis). If this level isn't present, more feed will be required to get the same results (particularly with young, growing horses).

Protein, while a crucial part of your horse's diet, has to be viewed in the proper perspective — as just one part of a working whole in the nutrition scheme. Now let's examine the inner workings of fiber.

Major Nutrient Requirements of Horses

Class of Horse (based on adult bodyweight of 500 kg)	Crude Protein (g)
Weanling at 4 months	669
Weanling at 6 months	676
Yearling (12 months)	846
Long yearling (18 months)	799
Two-year-old (24 months)	770
Mature horse — maintenance (idle)	630
Mature horse in light work (eg. pleasure riding)	699
Mature horse in moderate work (eg. jumping, cutting, ranch work)	768
Mature horse in intense work (eg. polo, racing, endurance)	1,004
Stallion in breeding season	789
Pregnant mare — first four months	630
Pregnant mare — eighth month	759
Pregnant mare — 11th month	893
Nursing mare — first month	1,535
Nursing mare — third month	1,468
Nursing mare — sixth month	1,265

From NRC (2006), 6th ed., Table 16-3 (Daily Nutrient Requirements of Horses, mature bodyweight 500 kg)

4

Fiber

Grazing is a full-time job for horses. Given their druthers, they would graze for 12 hours or more every day, their broad, flat teeth and sideways chewing motions making short work of the tough, stemmy grasses and weeds they favor. Like all true herbivores, horses get most of their daily energy requirements from eating plant fibers.

While we often provide grain and supplemental fats to our domestic horses to give them the energy to do hard work, it's important to remember that horses were meant to use fiber as fuel — and fiber remains the most important ingredient in every equine diet. It provides all the energy horses need for everyday maintenance metabolism: ordinary functions such as breathing, walking, grazing, and sleeping. Without adequate fiber the horse's digestive system doesn't function properly — it loses the ability to move food particles efficiently through the gut. Also, its ability to conserve water and electrolytes is compromised. Without fiber in the digestive system, high-carbohydrate feeds tend to "pack" in the gut as well. The result is a horse at risk for dehydration, colic, and laminitis (not to mention stable vices such as cribbing and wood chewing, which often develop when a horse's fundamental urge to chew is not satisfied).

Except in the most strenuous circumstances (such as two-year-olds in heavy race training), fiber always should make up at least 50% (by weight) of your horse's daily diet. And for the vast majority of adult horses, that percentage can be pushed considerably higher — even to 100% if the horse is an easy keeper and/or is not being asked to do work. The basic principle is this: Grain is an optional part of a horse's diet; roughage (fiber) is not.

Yet, ironically, horses can't digest fiber. In fact, no animal can digest fiber on its own. Animals don't produce the enzymes needed to break the beta bonds of polysaccharide fibers and make the nutrients within available for use. Fortunately, horses, like most other animals, have thousands of invisible allies — a population of intestinal bacteria that resides in the cecum and colon and is specially adapted to digest the fiber that horses cannot digest. Through a fermentation process, these gut flora produce the necessary enzymes to convert fiber to volatile fatty acids (VFAs) the horse can absorb. Not only do the bacteria benefit (making this a truly symbiotic relationship), but the VFAs they create provide between 30% and 70% of the horse's total digestible energy needs.

Assessing Fiber Quality

Not all fiber is created equal. Depending on its origins, it can vary widely in terms of quality and digestibility.

Fiber consists of three main substances: cellulose, hemicellulose, and lignin. Lignin is the very tough stuff that gives plant material its rigidity. (Oak trees are high in lignin; tender young grass shoots are low.) It is 100% indigestible by either horses or the bacteria they harbor in their digestive tracts. However, cellulose and, to a certain extent, hemicellulose are digestible, and it's from these materials that horses derive most of their digestible energy requirements.

Cellulose and hemicellulose are polysaccharide molecules, fairly complex chemical arrangements that need to be broken into smaller units to be absorbed through the gut wall. Breaking the "beta bonds" holding the individual monosaccharide molecules together allows their conversion to VFAs. Cellulose and hemicellulose, which stem from the non-seed and non-fruit portions of a plant, such as the leaves, stems, and hulls, also are known as insoluble fiber. Soluble fiber (which makes up a relatively minor portion of the fiber in a horse's diet) is fiber stemming from the "liquid" portions of a plant: the resin, sap, pectins, and mucilages.

All plant eaters use nearly all of the soluble fiber they ingest. But the degree of insoluble fiber that horses use varies. The sooner the bacteria go to work breaking the beta bonds, the greater the percentage of the fiber used by the horse. But even undigested insoluble fiber has its place in the equine diet. It helps maintain gut motility and function as well as prevent the too-quick consumption of carbohydrates, which are readily digested and which sometimes cause digestive upset if not "cushioned" by fiber in the colon.

In practice, it's not terribly important to know how much of the fiber provided by a plant is soluble. An enzymatic test does exist, but it's rarely used because the differences are not significant from a feeding point of view. There are, however, a few ways of defining the fiber content of a feed — each with its own pros and cons.

"Crude fiber" is the value most of us are used to seeing on feed labels or tags. It's an estimate of the total fiber in a feed, but it's not terribly accurate. The calculation that results in a crude fiber value tends to overestimate the non-fiber carbohydrate content of a feed and underestimate the cellulose portion. This also leads to an over-estimation of the feed's caloric content and, thus, its feeding value. The CF is a useful approximation but not much more.

Another value commonly used to express the fiber content of a feed is the NDF, or neutral detergent fiber. Unlike the CF, an NDF value includes almost all of the cellulose in a feed sample and more than 50% of the hemicellulose, but it also erroneously includes a high percentage of digestible starches in its calculations. Acid deter-gent fiber, or ADF, generally is considered the most accurate way of expressing fiber percentages. ADF not only removes starches from consideration but also removes most of the hemicellulose. Because horses use most of the hemicellulose in a feed, ADF analysis ends up being a measure of the cellulose plus the lignin and, therefore, results in an underestimation of the feed's insoluble fiber content and an overestimation of its energy content and feeding value. Nonetheless, it's the best available indicator of fiber digestibility.

CF, ADF, and NDF values all can be generated by doing a lab analysis of your feed, a service most feed companies and many universities provide. (More about how to take a representative sample in a moment.)

Finding Fiber

For the vast majority of horses around the world, pasture grasses and hay (dried grasses and legumes) are the most common sources for that all-important fiber fix, and rightly so, because horses have evolved to eat these plants.

The fiber content of pasture and hay can fluctuate according to the environment, time of year, soil, and stage of growth of the plants. Early spring pasture, with its tender young grass shoots, tends to be high in soluble fiber and low in lignin. Later in the summer the grasses are tougher and less "rich." Likewise, hay cut early in its growth cycle, before it has developed seedheads, tends to be lower in overall fiber than hay cut late; but early cut hay also is proportionately lower in lignin and higher in digestible

Pasture grass is a common source of fiber.

fiber. Once the plants have gone to seed, their stems tend to become tough and fibrous, and palatability and digestibility plummet.

By contrast, the fiber content of most grains doesn't vary a lot. Regardless of the stage of a plant's growth, you can pretty much depend on the fiber values of grains to be within the ranges listed in the chart on page 39. As a result, most horse owners can rely on the information on the feed tag and forego getting a fiber analysis of their grain ration. But doing an analysis of your hay (and/or pasture) can be valuable, especially as similar-looking batches of hay can be remarkably dissimilar in fiber content.

Analyzing hay can be valuable.

The best way to sample hay is by using a corer (ask your feed store to loan you the tool) on several bales. Insert the corer diagonally along the long axis of each of the bales rather than straight through the center, and take samples from at least 20 bales, ideally, mixing them together in a clean paper or plastic bag. If you don't have access to a corer, you also can get good results by doing a "grab sample," taking a handful of hay from 20 bales, each from different parts of the hay field. Make sure to get some from the center flakes and some from the ends to get a real mixture. The proportion of leaves to stems can make a big difference to the resultant ADF and NDF values, so make sure that you have not grabbed too much of one and not enough of another. Most labs can return results within a week or two at a cost of approximately $25 to $50.

If you want to get a fiber analysis of your pasture, first use a bit of observation. There is no point in analyzing the fiber content of plants your horses don't eat, so begin by watching them to see which plants they favor. Then take handfuls of only those plants from several locations throughout your field.

How do you interpret the results? As a rough guideline, forage with an acid detergent fiber value of more than 35% is considered poor quality and probably is past bloom. Its digestibility will be low which is not to say that it cannot be fed, but that you will have to feed considerably more of it for your horses to extract the same quantity of nutrients they could glean from a "younger" forage. (It's interesting to note that donkeys, which are adapted to living in harsh conditions, are considerably more efficient at extracting nutrients from poor-quality, highly indigestible forages than are horses and ponies.) ADF is considered a good overall parameter for assessing the maturity of forages.

Hay and pasture grasses are not the only fiber sources available to horses. One of the most popular alternatives is sugar beet pulp, a feed additive made from the fibrous portion of the sugar beet after the sugar has been extracted. Available in North America almost exclusively in a dehydrated format (either shredded or in pellet form), beet pulp can be rehydrated by soaking it in water for a few hours before feeding. (Studies have determined that soaking beet pulp is not actually necessary for a horse's digestive health. Horses fed varying quantities of dehydrated, unsoaked beet pulp demonstrated no ill effects — though many horsemen prefer soaking beet pulp to make the feed more palatable and reduce the risk of choke.)

Beet pulp has an ADF value of less than 28%, making it a very digestible fiber source and a useful supplement to hay or pasture for any of several circumstances. When beet pulp is soaked, its soft texture is easy to chew, making it a good choice for older horses or any animal with a dental problem. It also is favored for putting weight on "hard keepers," and it makes a convenient place to hide oral medications. Many horse people also serve it warm on cold winter nights, though one suspects that the comforting effect of such a meal does more for the owner's psyche than for the horse. Because the crude protein content of beet pulp is fairly low (averaging around 8%), it is appropriate for almost every type of horse. It is also fairly high in calcium.

Bran, another traditional way of supplementing fiber, is a less suitable choice. Bran is the grain kernel's outer layer that

Feeding bran mash is fine, but it is not the best fiber source.

is removed in the process of milling. Wheat bran is the type most commonly fed to horses (though rice bran is sometimes used as a fat supplement in small quantities). A fluffy, low-density feed, bran is only half as dense as (and thus delivers only half the digestible energy of) oats and only a quarter as dense, and energy rich, as corn or barley. So despite its ADF of approximately 15%, it takes a lot of bran to provide sufficient fiber for the average adult horse. Furthermore, its purported laxative effect has been shown to be a myth. Whether fed dry or wet, bran has no demonstrated "loosening" or "regulating" effect on the bowels. (The loose manure many owners observe after the feeding of a weekly bran mash is, in fact, the result of a mild digestive upset from a sudden change in the diet!) An occasional small bran mash probably does no harm, but as a fiber supplement, there are better choices. If you must feed bran, make it no more than 10% of your horse's total ration.

Two other fiber supplements are lignin rich and largely indigestible. They are added to the diet mostly as "busy food" — useful in keeping obese or idle horses chewing away — and, to some extent, to aid in digestive health by keeping gut motility up to speed. Chaff (chopped straw or low-quality hay) is a feed additive mixed in with grain that is often used in the United Kingdom. Chaff helps to slow down a horse that bolts its feed, to "fake out" an overweight or greedy horse that would like to be getting more grain than he needs, or to "cushion" the system of a horse with a tendency to colic. Oat straw and barley straw are commonly used to make chaff, and while their ADF values are usually more than 35%, they are certainly harmless even if they provide more bulk than nutrition to the diet.

Grain hulls are another inexpensive way to provide that same effect. High in crude fiber (up to 50% higher than grass hay) and low in energy, hulls can be used to replace some or all of the forage in a horse's diet. The hulls of most cereal grains can be fed safely to horses. Oat hulls are particularly popular, and coarsely ground corn cobs are another similar product. There is one caveat: Because hulls are often ground, they tend to be dusty. Blending them with a little water or molasses can help keep the dust down, or you can buy a pelleted version.

One downside to most of these alternate fiber sources is that the horse can consume them far faster than he can consume hay — so any time you substitute another fiber source for forage or pasture, you could be giving your horse less opportunity to satisfy his compelling urge to chew (which is part and parcel of his herbivorous nature). Boredom can translate that urge into stable vices, coprophagy (eating manure), even munching on the stall walls or his neighbor's tail.

Feeding small meals often (at least three to four times a day) is a partial solution. But under most circumstances, forage is still the best and most natural choice for most horses. Other fiber sources can be used as supplements to hay or pasture, or as a complete substitute only in cases such as advanced respiratory disease (i.e., heaves) or dental problems that make it impossible for the horse to chew and process forage.

For more on hay, take a look at Chapter 9.

Representative Fiber Values
for Common Horse Feeds

Feed	Crude Fiber (%)	Acid Detergent Fiber (ADF) (%)
Alfalfa, early hay	23	28.6
Alfalfa, late hay	30	39.5
Barley	6	7.2
Beet pulp	20	22-23
Bran, rice	13	13.1
Bran, wheat	10-12	13-15
Clover hay	21-31	32-36
Corn	2.5	3.4
Corn cobs, ground	35	42
Grass hay, early	31-34	31.4
Grass hay, late	31-35	41.6
Molasses	0-0.5	0.1-0.2
Oats	11-12	13.5-14.6
Oat hay	32	36.4
Oat hulls	33-36	40-44
Sorghum/milo	2.8	5.9
Soybean meal (44%)	7	10

From Lon D. Lewis's *Feeding and Care of the Horse* (1996), 2nd ed., and NRC (2006) 6th ed., Table 16-6 (Nutrient Composition of Selected Feedstuffs)

Energy and Carbs

If forages provide the "maintenance" energy horses need for the workings of everyday life — grazing, sleeping, wandering from pasture to pasture, maintaining internal temperature — then cereal grains are the turbo-charged portion of the diet. Their main function is to provide higher concentrations of energy, in the form of carbohydrates and starches, so that the horse can do the work we ask of him.

The amount of energy your horse needs rises in direct proportion to how fast, how long, and how hard you expect him to perform. At the lowest end of the spectrum are horses that are idle, or perhaps work only a few times a week at a very slow pace. Most pleasure horses and school horses fall into this category. At the opposite end are racehorses, which probably work harder than any other category of equine athlete (particularly because they're often asked for peak performance while they're still physically immature). Somewhere in between might be your equine athlete — whether he's a Western pleasure horse, a Grand Prix jumper, a polo pony, or one of a four-in-hand driving team. His energy requirements will more than likely not be completely met by hay or pasture alone.

Work isn't the only thing that can raise a horse's energy requirements above the maintenance level. Environmental conditions, his physical fitness, and his degree of fatigue all play roles. Even when all of these factors are identical, individuals can vary in their energy needs. We all know of high-strung horses that are "hard keepers" and their metabolic opposites, the easy-going types that maintain weight, even in hard work. Both breed type and temperament play roles here.

Pregnancy also places increased energy demands on the mare, especially in the latter half of gestation, when the fetus is developing most rapidly. Lactation and growth are two other situations in which energy needs are higher than usual.

Even a horse's size can have something to do with energy requirements. Studies have indicated that the energy requirement of horses at rest is proportional to the horse's bodyweight — so in theory, the energy requirement of a 500-pound pony is about half that of a 1,000-pound horse.

Unlocking the Energy

Carbohydrates and starches, contained in grains, are the most convenient ways to provide extra energy to your horse. A carbohydrate molecule is composed of simple sugars (also called monosaccharides) such as fructose, glucose, galactose, mannose, arabinose, and xylose. There are also disaccharides, which are two sugars bonded together. Lactose, made up of one glucose and one galactose molecule, is an important disaccharides for foals of nursing age.

Many glucose molecules, attached together by "alpha bonds," form the polysaccharides called starch (present in plants), and glycogen (present in animals). These two are sometimes called soluble or non-fiber carbohydrates, and both are readily used by the horse, providing much of his dietary energy. But other forms of carbohydrates contribute a substantial amount of "juice" as well. As we saw in the previous chapter, glucose molecules that are attached together by "beta bonds" instead of alpha bonds, form the polysaccharide cellulose (insoluble fiber). Likewise, hemicellulose is constructed of many molecules of the monosaccharide xylose, connected by beta bonds. So while we consider fiber and carbohydrates two entirely different things, they are really very closely related.

Monosaccharides are the only form of carbohydrate that can be absorbed from the intestinal tract, so the alpha or beta bonds of polysaccharides must be broken down in the gut before the horse can begin to use (or store) the simple sugars. The digestive enzyme amylase is responsible for this important job. All animals secrete amylase, primarily from the pancreas into the small intestine. Amylase takes care of the first step of carbohydrate digestion, breaking the polysaccharide molecules down into a disaccharide (a two-sugar molecule) called maltose. After that, the disaccharide enzyme maltase takes over and further breaks down maltose into its monosaccharide components. Two other digestive enzymes, lactase and sucrase, also might be called into play if lactose (milk sugar) or sucrose (table sugar) is present in the gut. (Lactase is usually present only in young, nursing horses and later becomes scarce enough that adult horses have difficulty digesting milk products and usually end up with diarrhea.) Because these enzymes emanate

Pregnant mares have higher energy needs.

from the interior intestinal wall, any damage to that area (as from enteritis, for example) results in impaired carbohydrate utilization. Large amounts of carbohydrates can remain in the gut, again causing diarrhea.

The simple sugars that pass through the intestinal wall are almost immediately available for energy use. Often, however, the energy isn't needed right at that moment, so the body busily begins re-assembling the sugars in the form of glycogen so they can be stored. Storage depots in the liver and muscles (and to a lesser extent, the kidneys) give the horse a substantial energy warehouse, and if these storage areas become full, any extra monosaccharides are then converted to and stored as fat. Both glycogen and fat can be drawn on for energy whenever they're needed (more on fats in the next chapter). The hormone insulin acts as a glucose regulator in the bloodstream, determining how much sugar remains there and how much gets stored.

Determining Dietary Energy

Not all the energy contained in a feed is accessible to the horse. A significant portion of it is lost in the conversion process of diges-tion. The digestible energy (DE) is the value most often used to describe the usable portion of the total energy, or gross energy. It consists of the portion of energy *not* lost in the feces. However, like many things in the nutritional world, it isn't perfect: The DE value doesn't take into account energy lost in urine (and to a lesser extent, in gastrointestinal gases such as methane), nor energy lost as heat in the actual digestion and absorption of the food. Nonetheless, DE values for foods are far easier to come by than values that do take these minor factors into account (which are far more difficult to calculate), so DE is the unit in common usage. Just keep in mind that when you see a DE value, it's likely to be a little generous.

Another way of calculating the energy content of feeds is by the familiar Calorie, the amount of heat generated by oxidation (burn-ing) to raise the temperature of a kilogram of water by one degree Celsius. (The capital-C calorie is actually shorthand for a kilocalo-rie; the original small-c calorie unit is the amount of heat required to raise the temperature of one gram of water one degree. It's too small a unit to be of practical use when discussing nutrition.) When dealing with horses and other large animals, nutritionists usually switch to the megacalorie (Mcal), which is 1,000 kilocalories. It saves writing a lot of zeros.

A third unit in common use is TDN, or total digestible nutrients, a measure of digestible energy expressed in either weight or percentages. TDN is the

sum of a feed's digestible carbohydrates, its digestible protein, and its digestible fats multiplied by 2.25 (because fats provide about 2.25 times more energy than carbohydrates or proteins). One kg TDN is approximately equal to 4.4 Mcal. (If you use TDN as the basis of your ration formulating, make sure you have

Light work includes Western pleasure.

a TDN value for horses, not ruminants, such as cattle. Ruminants are much more efficient digestion-wise than horses, so calculations for energy available from forages are generally 5% to 15% higher. If you formulate a ration for a horse based on ruminant TDN, you will likely be providing too little feed in the long run.)

A couple of formulas can help you calculate how much digestible energy your horse requires for his daily maintenance needs (without weight change).

For the average horse weighing less than 600 kg (1,320 lbs), use this formula:

Mcal DE/day = 1.4 + 0.03 x (kg body weight)

So for example, if your Standardbred mare weighs 450 kg (that's 990 pounds), she would require 1.4 + (0.03 x 450) Mcal, which equals 14.9 Mcal of digestible energy per day for her maintenance metabolism.

If your horses weigh more than 600 kg, they will have lower

energy needs per kilogram than smaller animals. So they have a slightly altered formula:

Mcal DE/day = 1.82 + (0.0383 x kg body weight) – [0.000015 x (kg body weight)^2]

Using this formula, a 750 kg Belgian gelding, for example, would require 1.82 + 28.73 – 8.44 = 22.11 Mcal/day.

You also can do rough calculations for how much additional energy your horse will need for various kinds of work. For ponies and light horses, the Mcal DE/day for light, medium, and intense work has been estimated at (respectively) 1.25, 1.5, and 2.0 times the amount needed for maintenance. What constitutes light, medium, or intense work? It depends, of course, on a number of factors, but generally speaking, light work includes such activities as Western or English pleasure, trail riding, quiet pleasure driving, and acting as a beginner level lesson horse. Medium work encompasses functions like ranch work, roping, cutting, jumping, barrel racing, and dressage. Intense work includes race training, polo, endurance riding, and upper-level three-day eventing.

Three-day eventing constitutes intense work.

Given the opportunity and good health, horses will choose to consume enough feed to meet their energy needs as a rule. Four things can contribute to a horse's not getting enough energy:

1) A sufficient quantity of food is not available;

2) His gastrointestinal tract will not hold enough of the available feed because the DE density of the feed is too low (as with poor-quality hay, for example);

3) He can't consume enough because of a physical problem (such as an injury or dental problem);

4) He doesn't want to consume the feed because illness, stress, unpalatable feed, or inadequate water intake has left him with no appetite.

Regardless of the reason, the first sign of inadequate energy intake is a depressed attitude. Eventually, hormonal changes will decrease the body's energy utilization, shutting down growth in youngsters or milk production in broodmares, and reducing physical activity. These changes also will call on the system to draw on stored fats and carbohydrates, resulting in weight loss. The horse's stores of carbohydrates are depleted within the first few days of total food deprivation, and within a week the body adapts, drawing on body fat and conserving the body protein.

But if starvation continues, the horse will have no choice but to turn to his structural protein for energy once the fat stores are depleted. First, proteins in the blood, intestines, and muscle are drawn on, followed by those lending structural support to bones, ligaments, tendons, and cartilage. By the time muscle wasting or weakness is evident, feed-deprivation-induced changes in other body functions are already well under way. The good news is that providing adequate calories usually can reverse the damage over time.

Far more common, fortunately, with domestic horses at least, is an energy excess. Horses that routinely receive too much feed will develop increased fat stores for a start. Some of the excess energy also will be given off as heat (a mechanism used by many animals, including humans); but the horse is unique in that he also compensates for excess energy intake by increasing his physical activity. The result is familiar to many of us: a snorting, shying, bucking explosion looking for a place to happen! In the young horse, excess energy also contributes to rapid growth, which can sometimes increase the risk of developmental orthopedic (bone and joint) problems. Reducing the amount of feed, especially grains, in the diet and providing more outlets for exercise usually will take care of this problem.

Carbs and Work

As we've noted, one of the best reasons for feeding your horse concentrated carbs is to fuel his ability to work over and above his normal maintenance metabolism. He can store the energy from grains in long glucose chains called glycogen and call on these chains to power his performance.

During exercise the horse's muscle fibers can tap into energy from muscle glycogen stores, from circulating blood glucose, or from stores in the liver. The longer the exercise interval and the more intense the exercise, the more glycogen gets used up. When strenuous exercise continues for some time, the horse's muscle and liver glycogen stores can become seriously depleted, so maintaining carbohydrate availability is important, particularly for horses asked to do sustained work, such as endurance racing. Being asked to work hard with depleted glycogen stores hastens the onset of fatigue in these horses, though the effects of diminished glycogen stores on the performance of short-term, high intensity athletes is less well understood.

The ability to replace depleted glycogen stores following exercise can be important for succeeding performance efforts, and some evidence suggests that the best time to do that is in the first few hours following an athletic effort. (Feeding both hay and grain post-exercise seems to do a better job of refilling glycogen stores than feeding hay alone.)

Delivering the Goods

Supplying your horse with energy-rich carbohydrates is as easy as running down to the feed store and picking up a bag of grain. Or is it? All grains contain large amounts of carbohydrates and starches, but not all grains are equivalent. Here's what they have in common: Grains are four to eight times as heavy as baled hay (per unit volume); they're low in fiber and about 50% higher in dietary energy than average-to-good quality hay; and starch makes up 55% or more of their dry matter.

Grains with seed coats, such as oats, tend to be somewhat lower in carbohydrates and higher in fiber than hull-less seeds such as corn, which are very carbohydrate dense. On the whole, starch digestibility by the horse is high — researchers estimate that the average horse uses from 87% to 100% of the starch he's given. And therein lies a problem. When a large grain meal hits the horse's

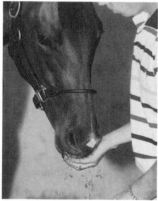

Grain is a source of carbohydrates.

small intestine, some of the starch is digested and absorbed as simple sugars, as it's meant to be, but the rest, instead of passing through the system undigested, is converted by the microflora in the cecum to volatile fatty acids and lactic acid. If the production of these acids is rapid enough (as can happen when a horse gets a large grain meal at one sitting — or when he breaks into the feed room and gorges), cecal acidosis can result — a condition that can trigger diarrhea, colic, and laminitis.

To reduce the risk of this reaction, it's wise to follow the old horseman's credo of "small meals often." This gives the small intestine time to process the carbohydrates before the system moves everything along to the cecum. The more carbohydrates get in the small intestine, the less cecal acidosis. Because forage in the system can decrease the amount of grain processed in the small intestine, it's best not to feed hay for an hour or more before feeding grain or for three or more hours afterward — though this rule is more important for high-performance horses routinely receiving large amounts of carbohydrates than for the average pleasure horse eating only a small amount of supplemental grain.

Other approaches that can help include giving preference to grains with fiber-rich hulls, such as oats, or choosing grains processed by grinding, rolling, flaking, or heat treatment to improve the digestibility of the starches. (More on choosing grains in Chapter 10.)

The Glycemic Index

When a horse consumes a meal high in starches, his blood glucose concentrations rise. In response, insulin levels also rise, stimulating muscle and fat tissues to take up and store the glucose for future use.

In humans, the term "glycemic index" is used to describe the level of the blood glucose increase to various foods. Several studies have attempted to apply the glycemic index to horse feeds, but it has been difficult to standardize the methods and the foods used to stimulate an increase in blood glucose. Other factors, such as the breed, age, and fitness level of the horse, and the feed format, would also have to be taken into account before the glycemic index can become a useful value in equine nutrition.

Grain	Digestible Energy (Mcal/kg)
Oats (regular)	3.2
Oats (heavy)	3.3
Corn (cracked or steam-flaked)	3.9
Barley (rolled)	3.7
Sorghum/milo	3.75
Wheat	3.8
Rye	3.4
Linseed meal	2.85
Millet	3.0
Soybeans, whole	3.35
Sunflower meal	2.4
Wheat bran	3.2
Rice bran	3.35
Molasses	4.0

From *Feeding and Care of the Horse* (1996), 2nd ed., by Lon D. Lewis, Ph.D., Dipl. ACVN. (Page 71, Table 4-5) and NRC (2006), 6th ed., Table 16-5 (Nutrient Composition of Selected Feedstuffs)

Feeding Fats

If there's a nutritional buzzword for the 21st century, it's fat. We humans still might not understand fully the differences between saturated and unsaturated fats, let alone "good" cholesterol and "bad" cholesterol — but we all know how to count our fat grams! While we struggle to keep our diets as low-fat as possible, fat has a different focus when it comes to the horse ... because only in recent years have we recognized the value of *raising* the fat levels in an equine athlete's diet.

Of course, the average human diet (at least in North America) contains far more than the maximum 30% fat recommended for good health. In contrast, the horse's natural diet contains almost no fat at all. Forages and fibers contribute none, and most grains fed to horses only contain between 2% and 3.5% fat overall. While this leaves the horse at low risk for cardiovascular clogging, it does mean that, traditionally, carbohydrates have been considered the obvious and "natural" energy source for performance horses, and fat has rarely been considered beyond that little splash of corn oil that's considered good for a shiny coat. Only in the past couple of decades have we begun to realize that fat is also a valuable energy source — one with many advantages.

High-fat diets (anything over and above the 2% to 3.5% supplied by a standard grain-plus-forage diet) provide several perks, most notably in terms of energy production for high-level equine performance. Pound for pound, fat supplies almost two and a half times as much energy as the equivalent weight of carbohydrates or starches (traditionally supplied by grains such as oats, corn, or barley). If you wish to supply more energy to your horse without significantly increasing his overall feed intake, supplementing the fat in his diet can be an excellent way to accomplish that.

Also, horses easily metabolize fat despite the fact that their digestive systems (best adapted for the processing of fiber) didn't really evolve to deal with it. Studies have shown that as much as 20% overall fat in the diet is well tolerated by horses, with no ill effects noted. Indeed, fat might be easier for horses to digest than carbohydrates. It has been demonstrated that a fat-supplemented diet, unlike a high-carbohydrate diet, has no effect on the pH of the cecum (and thus no detrimental effect on the beneficial microflora inhabiting the large intestine). Fat appears to be absorbed almost exclusively in the small intestine.

Another interesting fat digestion fact is that horses can use fats well despite having no gallbladder. In most mammals the gallbladder excretes bile and salts to help break down fats, but in horses the liver seems to take over that function, with no fat digestion problems that research has been able to identify.

Fat-supplemented diets also have been shown to decrease the amount of energy used for heat production in the horse's body. This decreases the horse's heat load and increases the amount of energy available for physical activity. In one study, where horses ate a fat-supplemented diet, the horse's total body heat production decreased by 14%, and the diet had no effect on the amount of energy needed for maintenance metabolism, therefore leaving more energy available for performance requirements (or for energy storage in the form of glycogen or fat). The end result was that more than 60%

greater energy was available for physical activity (regardless of what the ambient temperature was or how skinny or plump the horse was at the time).

Some of the most compelling research behind fat demonstrates a fat-supplemented diet's benefits for high-performance horses (in sports such as three-day eventing, racing, polo, endurance racing, and cutting). But to understand how fat acts as a performance enhancer, we first have to understand some exercise physiology basics.

Dietary Fat for Athletic Performance

Grains, the "traditional" feed for high-level physical activity, supply carbohydrates and starches — versatile energy substrates that fuel the horse's muscles for athletic endeavors of all kinds. Fat is also an energy substrate, which while not as flexible as carbohydrates in terms of the types of activities it can fuel, might in many ways help the horse's body use itself with more efficiency and less fatigue.

Two main energy pathways fuel a horse's muscle cells to do work. (A third pathway, called "anaerobic alactic" metabolism, is a "start-up" system that only comes into play for bursts of hundredths of a second.) The predominant energy pathway is aerobic metabolism, which the muscles use whenever they can, for all low-intensity and endurance activities, especially those requiring a continuous effort of longer than two minutes (and possibly lasting many hours). Blood glucose, derived from carbohydrates and starches when they are broken down in the gut, is the main energy substrate for aerobic metabolism, and muscle cells will draw on blood glucose as needed. Oxygen, from the lungs, is the "fuel" used to burn the glucose to produce ATP (adenosine triphosphate, the "energy molecule") along with the non-toxic by-products, water and carbon dioxide.

Blood glucose levels are regulated by insulin, which responds to high blood-glucose levels (as happens two to three hours after a high-carbohydrate meal) by increasing and converting excess glucose to glycogen, the form in which it is stored in muscle, fat, and liver cells. Another hormone, glucagon, can reverse the process, converting glycogen back into glucose and releasing it into the blood. This mechanism, while efficient, is not foolproof — sometimes insulin might "spike" in response to a large load of carbohydrates being introduced, causing large amounts of blood glucose to be converted to glycogen and stored away. This can leave a horse hypoglycemic (low in blood sugar) and feeling weak and fatigued.

Sprint activities such as pole bending are fueled by anaerobic metabolism.

As long as a horse stays below a certain performance threshold (which can vary somewhat depending on the horse's activity, his conformation and muscle bulk, and his degree of fitness), he can work aerobically. It's essentially a "clean-burning" system that horses can maintain indefinitely, as long as fuel continues to come in on a regular basis. Thus, it's the least taxing to the system — but as blood glucose drops and as glycogen is drawn upon and then depleted, fatigue can set in and force the horse's body to switch to another energy pathway.

During high-intensity exercise of short duration, or when glycogen depletion no longer allows a horse to work aerobically, his muscles will use anaerobic lactic metabolism. "Sprint" type activities of about ten seconds to two minutes in length are typical "anaerobic" activities; barrel racing is a good example. When the aerobic system is working close to its full capacity, the anaerobic system also will "kick in" like a supercharger, augmenting rather than replacing the aerobic metabolism.

The anaerobic lactic system is entirely dependent on stored glycogen in the muscles as an energy source. It is a far less efficient system than aerobic metabolism in terms of the ATP produced per molecule of glycogen, and so it depletes glycogen rapidly.

Here's where fat (finally!) comes in. Fat broken down in the digestive tract becomes fatty acids — which can fuel aerobic metabolism but not anaerobic. Adding fat to the diet provides a second source with which the body can continue to work aerobically, delaying the switchover to anaerobic metabolism and thus postponing fatigue and performance deficits.

High-fat diets can help horses in high-speed activities

Studies have indicated that if the horse's system has supplemental levels of fat available as an energy source, it can "learn" to use it in preference to glycogen, thus increasing the amount of muscle glycogen the horse maintains. That's good, because while glycogen stores in the body are limited, fat (in the form of stored short-chain volatile fatty acids, or VFAs) is the most abundant energy source in the body. Horses fed a high-fat diet also appear to have better muscle glycogen utilization during anaerobic (sprint-type) activities and no change in their blood glucose concentration (and thus their insulin concentration) while working anaerobically. During aerobic (endurance-type) activity, the same horses showed less decrease in their blood glucose concentration than did horses fed a traditional grain diet, and there was muscle glycogen sparing (less utilization of stored glycogen). This glycogen sparing helps delay fatigue, an important factor in performance enhancement. As a racing sage once observed, it isn't so much which horse is going the fastest at the end of the race — it's more about which horse is slowing down the least!

Pros and Cons

Horses fed high-fat diets (15% added soy oil) appear to perform better than those fed either a high-starch diet (40%) or a high-protein diet (25%) for both high-speed (racing) activities, and moderate-speed activities (fast trot/slow canter speeds of about five meters a second). Their blood glucose levels decreased less, and for a shorter duration, than did those horses on high-carb diets. These benefits might produce only subtle results — but even a gain of a few feet on a racetrack might result in a Derby win. Even at lower levels of performance, the change can be valuable. For example, a low goal polo player might find that his horse can recover more quickly and, perhaps, be able to play one more chukker than before.

That's not to say that fat is a miracle ingredient. For reasons we don't yet fully understand, the horse's body must "learn" to use fat as an energy source, a process requiring considerable metabolic adaptation on the part of the muscle cells. It can take three to four weeks, and the blood chemistry might continue to adapt for up to six weeks. What this means is that you can't just start feeding fat the day of the big race and see results. Not only do you have to put your horse on the fat-supplemented diet a good month in advance, but you also have to challenge his system so that it begins to adapt. For a racehorse, that means you have to race him on the new diet, not just train him conservatively, to help him begin to assimilate the new energy source.

And as nice as it might be to contemplate improving further on the benefits of feeding fat by feeding greater amounts — perhaps eliminating grain altogether — unfortunately, it just doesn't work that way. Remember that only carbohydrates can fuel the anaerobic system of metabolism, which all horses use to some degree in their work — and that forages alone provide a minimum of carbohydrate. (Fed by itself, forages provide plenty of fuel for maintenance metabolism but not enough for the vast majority of horses to do the work we ask.) Grain in the diet is an important fuel source for any performance horse, and study after study has confirmed that high-fat diets work best in conjunction with fairly high-grain diets, for maximum benefit in hard-working horses (such as 100-mile endurance racers, Thoroughbred and Standardbred racehorses, and upper-level three-day-event horses). The exception is horses with a genetic defect called equine polysaccharide storage myopathy (EPSM), which have difficulty using carbohydrates as an energy substrate; a prescribed diet in which fats almost completely replace grains usually allows these horses to continue to perform (more on EPSM in Chapter 12).

So what level of fat is optimum for a performance benefit? That number is still under debate. Some researchers now recommend a level of 10% (by weight) of the total daily diet for horses working at the extreme end of the athletic spectrum, though slightly lower levels (about 8%) might be more appropriate for horses working at a lower level of intensity. The level of fat you choose might depend somewhat on the activity you're asking your horse to perform. Some studies have indicated that levels up to 15% are beneficial for horses involved in intense, long-term endurance activities (chiefly competitive trail and endurance racing, and upper-level three-day-eventing). However, even a level of 6% to 8% will result in some performance benefit for horses involved in more moderate activity.

Feeding fat can also be well worth considering for reasons other than performance enhancement — good news for the vast majority of us, who are dealing with horses *not* at the cutting-edge of high performance.

First, it's true that supplemental levels of fat can enhance the quality and shine of the hair coat, giving your horse a healthy glow that reflects particularly well in the show ring. Supplemental fat also can help put or keep weight on a "hard keeper," provided he is not in heavy work. Just as we do (far too efficiently, sometimes!), horses will store excess fat in the adipose tissues — so for plumping up a skinny horse, added fat is an excellent solution that carries far less risk of stomach upset and other complications than does a switch to a high-carbohydrate diet.

As the condition of their teeth starts to deteriorate and their digestive efficiency wanes, older horses might benefit from a high-fat diet, too. Easily digested fat can help prevent them from losing condition and becoming ribby.

By the same token, broodmares can reap the rewards of added fat. Studies have indicated that a mare that has recently "gained some condition" (easily achieved by feeding added fat for a month or two before breeding) might

High-fat diets can benefit older horses.

catch more easily and maintain her pregnancy with less difficulty. In addition, a high-fat diet can help her deal with the stress of lactation, which can be considerable. A third perk is that her milk will be higher in fat (mare's milk being fairly low to begin with), and as a result her foal will tend to gain weight and condition more easily.

Fat is often touted as an ingredient that provides energy without the "hotness" that carbohydrates provide — so it is sometimes recommended in an effort to calm a hot horse. Unfortunately, this one is a myth. As experts in both human and equine research have noted, carbohydrates are falsely accused of causing a "sugar high," so substituting fat for a portion of the grain being fed will make no difference to a horse's temperament or attitude. The idea of horses getting "hot" from high-grain diets has more to do with their being in hard training at the same time their grain ration is increased, than it does with any physiological effects on a horse's manners. As most trainers know, when you're exercising vigorously, you feel good and you have more energy. The fact that you're getting more groceries is coincidental.

How To Feed Fat

Adding fat to your horse's diet can be done in a number of ways. Practically any digestible source of fat, either vegetable or animal, might be used. The only source to avoid is the rumen-protectant variety of fat designed for cattle, which horses will find at best indigestible and at worst, toxic. (You won't run into this one unless you ask for it specifically at the feed store.) It's interesting to note that horses actually can digest fat from animal sources (such as tallow) very well, despite their vegetarian innards. From an economic standpoint, animal-fat products are generally much less expensive than comparable vegetable fats or oils. But animal fats are seldom used in horse rations for two reasons: First, they are usually solids at room temperature, so they must be heated to liquid to mix with a grain ration; and second, their palatability is generally low (try to get a horse to eat something that smells like bacon grease!).

Of the vegetable sources of fats (which usually come in the form of oils), corn and soy oil are traditional favorites and are readily available at most feed mills as well as at many supermarkets. Other vegetable oils are just as suitable, however, although many horse owners avoid canola oil as its palatability isn't as good. Top-dressing your horse's grain ration with oil is a simple process of measuring and pouring — but like any feed additive, it should be introduced gradually, over two to three weeks.

Other feed additives that are relatively high-fat, most notably rice bran, have gained considerable popularity in parts of the United States. Rice bran products, which come either as a powder or as an extruded pellet, are approximately 22% fat, which means you have to feed considerably more rice bran to get the same benefits as you would from a 100% fat product such as vegetable oil. Rice bran has the advantage of being much more stable, however, and is often preferred in warm, humid climates where oils and animal fats tend to go rancid very quickly. Extruded soybeans, another high-fat product, are good for young growing horses because they are also a good protein source. For that same reason, they're not as appropriate for mature animals. Then there's flax seed (30% fat), which because of its omega-3 content is an increasingly popular option. However, flax seed's small, hard seed coat means it needs to be processed immediately with a coffee grinder before feeding to make the fats available for digestion. Or you can provide some extra fat with black-oil sunflower seeds (the unstriped kind, a.k.a. BOSS), which many horses relish as a treat. Sunflower seeds contain between 25% and 40% fat.

One of the simplest ways to add fat to your horse's diet is to choose a commercial grain ration that is fat supplemented. Many feed companies now offer these products, usually as part of their premium line. Fat-supplemented feeds are often equipped with extra anti-oxidants to prevent spoilage, a management perk, and have camouflaged the fats with other ingredients so there is no loss of palatability. Any feed that contains more than about 3.5% fat is considered to be fat supplemented. Look for a crude fat level of 8% to 10% on the label (and if your horse is a mature animal not being used for breeding, a protein content of 10% to 12% at most), and introduce it gradually to your horse's diet. If your horse objects to top-dressed oil or rice bran, the best way to go might be a fat-supplemented sweetfeed or pellet.

However you decide to add fat to your horse's diet, you must consider how it will affect the overall nutrient balance of his daily ration. If you add fat to your horse's routine but don't increase his exercise level or cut down on his grain, he's likely to get fat. However, if you cut back on your horse's grain, you also reduce the concentration of vitamins and minerals. In contrast to other feeds, oils contribute no incidental nutrient value — that is, they contain no protein, calcium, phosphorus, or any other nutrients to speak of beyond the fat calories, though other fat sources such as rice bran are sometimes supplemented. For this reason, it's important to work with an equine nutritionist (whom you can contact through your feed dealer, local veterinary college, or state extension service) to help you make the necessary adjustments so that your horse doesn't get cheated out of essential vitamins and minerals. You might have to consider adding a supplement to compensate for these losses.

If you're feeding a commercial ration that is a "premium" product, you might not have to worry about deficiencies of vitamins and minerals as many of these are deliberately designed with an excess of most nutrients. And if you decide to go with an all-inclusive high-fat feed, the feed company has likely already done the ration balancing for you. Consult with your equine nutritionist to be sure.

One thing fat is not going to do is make feeding any cheaper. Pound for pound, it usually works out to be nearly as expensive, if not a little more so, than a comparable quantity of carbohydrates. Is it cost-effective? That's hard to say. But as one researcher points out — if you can move a racehorse up six feet in a mile and a half, it doesn't really matter what it costs, does it?

Omega-3 and Omega-6

We've all been bombarded in recent years with information about the health benefits of "the omegas" — fatty acids that are supposed to bolster the immune system and help treat everything from heart disease to hemorrhoids. Are omega-3 fatty acids as important in an equine diet as they seem to be for humans? How about omega-6?

Omega-3 fatty acids are derived from alpha-linolenic acid, a polyunsaturated fat that must be sourced from the diet (the sources appropriate for horses include canola, sunflower, and soybean oils, and flax seeds, a.k.a. linseed). In several species, including humans, omega-3s have contributed to decreased inflammatory responses. Anecdotal evidence also supports their use in alleviating the symptoms of osteoarthritis, reducing allergic hypersensitivities, and easing exercise-induced bronchial constriction. Two varieties of omega-3 fatty acids often seen on food labels are EPA (eicosapentaenoic acid) and DHA (docosahexaenoic acid).

Omega-6 fatty acids, in contrast, come from linoleic acid, another polyunsaturated fat found in horse-friendly sources such as corn, safflower, and cottonseed oil, and black-oil sunflower seeds. They have the opposite effect of omega-3s: they increase the inflammatory response, aggravate allergic hypersensitivity, and increase bronchial constriction during exercise. That's why the emphasis is usually on delivering more omega-3 fatty acids in the diet and reducing the omega-6s — although omega-6 fatty acids are also essential and necessary nutrients. Not all inflammation is bad, after all. It's a process needed to fight infection and heal injured tissues. And the relatively minor percentage of fat that horses consume, as compared to that consumed by humans, means that omega-6 fatty acids have a relatively minor impact on their overall health.

Preliminary research in horses has yielded mixed results for omega-3 supplementation. In one study DHA failed to mitigate pulmonary inflammation and exercise-induced bleeding in racehorses, though in another study, horses on an omega-3 supplemented diet had reduced inflammatory responses to exercise. There's some good early evidence that DHA supplementation has the potential to improve sperm quality and quantity in stallions and improve its ability to withstand cooling and shipping. And, through their milk, mares fed supplemental corn oil (rich in omega-6) or a 50-50 mix of corn and linseed oil (rich in omega-3) passed along higher fatty acid levels to their foals, though the jury's still out as to whether that benefited the immune response in the babies. Much more work needs to be done before we really understand the pros and cons of "the omegas."

CHAPTER 7

Vitamins

Vitamins are tiny organic compounds with a huge impact on the health and well being of your horse. Sometimes gleaned from the diet and sometimes manufactured within the digestive tract, vitamins have the power to promote and regulate virtually all of the body's normal functions, and they need be present only in minute amounts.

Researchers have classified vitamins into two categories that describe how the vitamins are absorbed, stored, and excreted by the body: fat soluble and water soluble. Vitamins A, D, E, and K are fat-soluble vitamins, which tend to be stored in the body (and thus can build up toxicities if there is an excess), while the B vitamins and vitamin C are water soluble, meaning any excess not used quickly by the body tends to be excreted rather than stored.

Vitamins also can be classified according to their source. Under normal conditions, the horse quite efficiently produces his own vitamins C, D, and niacin (one of the B-complex vitamins) from other organic molecules he ingests. The beneficial microbes living in his cecum and large intestine, as part of their symbiotic bargain, produce all of the other B vitamins as well as vitamin K. Only vitamins A and E are not produced within the horse's body and must be obtained from vegetable matter in the diet.

We still don't know much about vitamins, and much of what we do know is misunderstood. One of the most common misconceptions about vitamins is that "if some is good, more is better."

Horses can become vitamin deficient, and these deficiencies can have devastating effects on their normal functions, but equally dangerous are toxicities from an overdose — a real possibility with some (but not all) of the vitamins. Furthermore, different species have different vitamin requirements, so assumptions extrapolated from human medicine might not necessarily apply to horses. Vitamin requirements don't really vary with the amount of work a horse does, either — the pleasure horse and high-performance athlete have almost identi-

cal needs. And while we frequently succumb to marketing ploys designed to convince us that our horses are in need of supplemental vitamins in their diet, the reality is that horses usually receive an excellent daily dose of the vitamins they require — those they cannot manufacture for themselves — from their forage (pasture or hay).

Vitamin excesses or deficiencies actually extreme enough to cause symptoms are pretty rare in horses. That's not to say however, that every diet provides absolutely optimum levels of vitamins. It's quite possible for a horse to be receiving enough vitamins for maintenance metabolism but not for maximum beneficial health effects.

For example, a real vitamin E deficiency only occurs when a horse takes in less than 10 to 15 International Units (IU) per kilogram of his bodyweight in the dry diet. This is a level easily exceeded by most feeds. But studies have demonstrated that a higher level of vitamin E, along the lines of 50 to 100 IU/kg (more than is delivered by most feeds), might increase a horse's resistance to infections and to exertion-induced muscle damage. This is a case where some supplementation might produce a beneficial effect over and above what's required nutritionally. Biotin, which we'll discuss more in a minute, is another vitamin often fed in excess of the amounts a horse strictly requires to live because it's reputed to have a beneficial effect on hoof growth and quality. But it's important to realize that in some cases, such effects might be more old-horseman's lore than fact. Research is ongoing, and each vitamin must be considered individually before you do any supplementing.

Should You Supplement?

Vitamin supplementation might be beneficial in the following:

• For horses on a high-grain, low-forage diet (such as youngsters in heavy race training), or for those on very poor-quality forage or eating hay that is more than a year old. Vitamins tend to break down over time in stored feed. For example, there is a 9.5% loss of vitamin A activity in hay every month.

• For horses receiving prolonged antibiotic treatment for illness or infection. Broad-spectrum antibiotics inhibit the growth of the beneficial cecal and intestinal bacteria, which inhibit their production of B vitamins and vitamin K.

• For horses in high-stress situations, such as frequent traveling, showing, or racing.

• For horses who are eating poorly — for example, those recovering from surgery or illness.

• For horses who are anemic — although the source of the anemia should be determined and treated first.

Vitamins in feed can decompose when exposed to sunlight, heat, air, or the processes that feed goes through in commercial packaging (such as grinding or cooking). Losses during long-term feed storage are greatest for vitamins A, D, K, and thiamin (B_1). Vitamin A is the most crucial of these because the horse does not manufacture it within his own system. Furthermore, some vitamins are incompatible with each other or with minerals that might also be in the feed. For example, most vitamins are prone to oxidative destruction by iron, copper, sulfates, sulfides, phosphates, and carbonates, all of which might be present in a feed or a vitamin/mineral supplement. The B vitamin thiamin (B_1) is incompatible with riboflavin (B_2), and both are incompatible with cobalamin (B_{12}) in the presence of light. So feed manufacturers might go to great lengths to protect the vitamins' activity and efficacy by coating them with gelatin, wax, sugar, or ethylcellulose — harmless, fortunately, to the horse in the amounts required. These compounds might compose a large part of a powdered or pelleted vitamin/mineral supplement. (Interestingly, it's very difficult to cover vitamins with any sort of protective coating in a liquid format, so many of the liquid supplements rich in B vitamins, iron, and copper, sold as "blood builders," might actually have very little active vitamin content.)

Fat-Soluble Vitamins

Here's a primer on the function of each of the vitamins important to the horse, beginning with the fat-soluble vitamins.

VITAMIN A

Function: Vitamin A, also called retinol, is important for maintaining good vision, particularly at night. It is also important in bone and muscle growth of young horses, in reproduction, and in healthy skin. New research has revealed that vitamin A has a key role in the immune response to infection as well.

Sources: Horses must satisfy all of their daily vitamin A requirements from their diets. Fortunately, green forages and yellow vegetables (such as carrots) are excellent sources of vitamin A's main precursor, beta-carotene, which is broken down by enzymes in the small intestine. The converted vitamin A is then stored in the liver, which can retain a three- to six-month supply, releasing it back into the bloodstream as the horse's body requires (or excreting it if there is an excess).

Not all of the carotenoid pigments the horse takes in on a daily basis are converted to vitamin A; some are absorbed intact and transported to body tissue such as the fat, skin, and ovaries for use and storage. (In the ovaries, beta-carotene has been shown to be involved in the control of progesterone secretion by the corpus luteum, making it a key player in the control of ovulation, embryo implantation, and the maintenance of pregnancy.) A deficiency of beta-carotene interferes with these functions, and, interestingly, cannot be corrected by feeding more vitamin A, as the conversion doesn't seem to be wholly reversible.

Feed companies may supplement their products with vitamin A in the form of retinyl-palmitate or retinyl-acetate, which are more stable than retinol and less vulnerable to degradation over time. These forms are converted to retinol in the small intestine just like beta-carotene.

Signs of deficiency: General signs of a vitamin A deficiency include a depressed appetite, weight loss, a dull haircoat, night blindness (distinguishable from periodic ophthalmia, or moon blindness, by characteristically cloudy corneas), excessive tearing of the eyes, anemia, and even convulsive seizures. Long-term deficiencies might cause abortion in broodmares, and stallions might suffer decreased libido and soft, flabby testicles. Under normal conditions, the only way a horse can develop a vitamin A deficiency is if he is deprived of hay or pasture for more than six months (allowing time to deplete the stores in the liver). But if horses are to be fed on very old hay or poor pasture for an extended period, vitamin A supplementation is a good idea.

Like all of the fat-soluble vitamins, vitamin A is poorly transported across the placenta. Thus, foals are born vitamin A-deficient. Provided the mare's diet has sufficient beta-carotene, she will provide vitamin A to her foal in her colostrum, but if the foal's colostrum intake is insufficient, the deficiency will persist. Vitamin A-deficient foals might suffer from diarrhea, though they are not usually night blind.

Signs of Toxicity: Horses can experience vitamin A toxicity; however, as a rule, it only occurs when an owner over-supplements the diet. In one study where foals were deliberately fed vitamin A in quantities exceeding 20,000 IU/kg, the results included stunted growth, scaly skin, increased bone size, bone fragility, and decreased blood clotting, leading to internal hemorrhages. There has been no demonstrated benefit to horses by feeding more than 2,000 to 3,000 IU/kg per day. For idle adult horses, 30 IU/kg per day is considered the maintenance vitamin A requirement; growing youngsters and pregnant or lactating mares might need double that.

VITAMIN D

Function: Vitamin D assists in maintaining plasma calcium concentrations by interacting with parathyroid hormone (PTH) and calcitonin. This has the effect of increasing the absorption of both calcium and phosphorus from the intestine. It also assists with mobilizing stored calcium, with an indirect impact on bone mineralization. Recent research indicates that vitamin D also influences cell growth and differentiation. (Differentiation is the process by which an unspecialized cell becomes specialized into one of the many cells that make up the body, such as a heart, liver, or muscle cell.)

Sources: Vitamin D is the "sunshine vitamin," created through chemical reactions of ultraviolet rays from the sun with 7-dehydro-cholesterol (synthesized in the horse's skin) and ergosterol (in the dead leaves of plants). Because chlorophyll in living plants blocks out ultraviolet rays, vitamin D begins to be present only after plants have been cut and exposed to sunlight (as in sun-cured hay).

Signs of Deficiency: A vitamin D deficiency results in rickets in the young of most species (including humans). The bones become soft and bendable, resulting in bowed legs and emaciation, and in severe cases the affected animal will be reluctant to stand. But rickets, per se, have not been observed in horses with vitamin D deficiencies. However, pony foals deprived of sunlight for five months did demonstrate decreased bone strength and slower growth and feed intake, as well as irregular growth plates (visible on radiographs).

Most horses are unlikely ever to need vitamin D supplementation. Hay contains approximately 2,000 IU/kg of vitamin D when it is freshly baled, though like all vitamins, it degrades over time, at a rate of about 7.5% per month. Hay more than a year old might not, therefore, meet a horse's vitamin D needs, but as long as the horse receives a few hours of sunlight a day, this should be of no consequence. However, stabled horses with no access to direct sunlight for months on end should have supplementation in their diets: 300 IU/kg (in the total diet) for normal maintenance or 800 IU/kg for growth, pregnancy, and lactation.

Signs of Toxicity: The most common of all vitamin "overdoses," vitamin D toxicity occurs as a result of indiscriminate supplementation (either oral or injectable). Excess vitamin D is stored in the liver, and the effects are cumulative, becoming more obvious after several weeks. They include calcium deposits that collect in the heart valves and walls, the walls of large blood vessels, and the kidney, diaphragm, salivary glands, and gastric mucosa. The result is decreased exercise tolerance, weight loss, stiffness, a decrease in spontaneous activity (with flexor tendons and suspensories often sensitive to palpation), an increased resting heart rate, the development of heart murmurs, and increased water intake and urination. Toxicosis can be confirmed by elevated plasma concentrations.

VITAMIN E

Function: Versatile vitamin E enhances immune function, is essential for cellular respiration, is involved in DNA synthesis, and improves the absorption and storage of vitamin A, among other effects. But most importantly, vitamin E and the mineral selenium are anti-oxidants and are partners in protecting the horse's body tissues — especially cell membranes, enzymes, and other intracellular compounds — from the damaging effects of oxidation. Inadequate amounts of either one in the horse's system assure considerable free-radical damage to the tissues.

Sources: Vitamin E is the only vitamin other than A that horses must source from their diets. Green growing forage contains good amounts of vitamin E, but from 30% to 80% of the vitamin's activity is lost during cutting and baling hay, and nearly all of the vitamin E is destroyed in high-moisture feeds such as haylage. Because not all horses are lucky enough to have good pasture year-round, commercial grain rations are usually fortified with stable forms of vitamin E (alpha-tocopheryl acetate is one).

Signs of Deficiency: Usually grouped with selenium deficiency, which we'll discuss in the next chapter, vitamin E deficiency can cause muscle wastage and malformation (sometimes called "white muscle disease" in foals); subcutaneous edema; infertility; a stiff, stilted "base wide" gait; a swollen tongue; and inflammation of fatty tissues, or steatitis, by insoluble pigments (often called "yellow-fat disease"), especially in foals. In horses aged two and up, prolonged vitamin E deficiency can contribute to equine motor neuron disease (EMND), which features the sudden onset of trembling, a constant shifting of the weight in the hind legs when standing, muscle wasting, and prolonged recumbency.

A mild deficiency of vitamin E might only produce a decrease in the horse's immune response and a slower growth rate in foals.

Signs of Toxicity: Horses can easily suffer from selenium excesses (selenium has the lowest toxicity level of any mineral important to the equine diet), but vitamin E appears to be safe for horses even at relatively high doses. Because of this, some feed manufacturers use it as a natural anti-oxidant in their grain rations to help prevent spoilage, leading to feed tag values that are far higher than the nutritional requirement of most horses.

No clinical signs of vitamin E toxicosis have been produced, but because very high levels can interfere with the absorption of other fat-soluble vitamins, a conservative maximum level of 1,000 IU/kg in the diet is generally recommended.

VITAMIN K

Function: Vitamin K is primarily an activator for blood clotting factors though it also participates in the activation of other proteins throughout the body. Bone metabolism and vascular (blood vessel) health also benefit from vitamin K.

Sources: Several forms of vitamin K occur in nature, some in green leafy plants and others manufactured by the horse's cecal bacteria. (There is also a synthetic form called menadione, used as a feed supplement and metabolized just like natural vitamin K.) While the natural forms of vitamin K are fat soluble, they are converted to a water-soluble format before they are stored in the horse's liver. As a result, vitamin K is easily excreted in the urine, so the body does not tend to retain a large supply. However, the combination of vitamin K ingested in pasture or hay, and that produced in the cecum, is considered adequate for any horse's needs under almost all circumstances.

One exception is a vitamin K deficiency induced by sweet clover poisoning. An anticoagulant called dicoumarol (chemically related to warfarin) sometimes occurs in moldy sweet clover hay or haylage. If the moldy hay is ingested over several weeks, the horse's synthesis of vitamin K-dependent clotting factors is impaired. The problem occurs most often in cattle but has been reported in both horses and sheep. If it is left untreated, mortality and the risk of abortion in broodmares can be high.

Vitamin K deficiencies also can result from anything that compromises the gut flora — such as severe colic or diarrhea, abdominal surgery, or antibacterial drugs. Chronic liver disease also can be a factor. And because newborn foals are deficient at birth, vitamin K injections often are recommended to prevent hemorrhagic diseases.

Signs of Deficiency: A long-term vitamin K deficiency decreases blood coagulation. Bleeding from the nose is frequently one of the first signs in horses. Hematomas and/or internal bleeding might also occur, and if sufficient blood is lost, the horse will have pale mucous membranes, a rapid and irregular heartbeat, and depression and weakness.

Signs of Toxicity: Vitamin K toxicity is rare, though injections of the water-soluble form can be dangerous, causing acute renal failure and death. Oral forms of the vitamin appear to be innocuous, fortunately. No ideal levels of vitamin K have been established for the horse, but in a case where supplementation is called for (for example, after a course of antibiotics or after a serious colic), the usual recommendation is for 3 to 5 mg/kg of body weight/day mixed into the feed for a week or more.

Water-Soluble Vitamins

THIAMIN (VITAMIN B₁)

Function: Thiamin plays an important role in carbohydrate metabolism and in nerve transmission and stimulation.

Sources: While horses do receive good concentrations of thiamin from their intestinal bacteria, several studies have determined that they also require some more from their diets. Fortunately, most green forage is an excellent source of thiamin (and indeed, all of the "B-complex" vitamins), as is brewer's yeast.

Signs of Deficiency: Thiamin deficiency can occur when horses eat bracken ferns (which contain a compound that inhibits the vitamin's absorption) but is otherwise uncommon. In studies where the deficiency has been artificially produced, horses showed signs of anorexia, loss of coordination, skipped heartbeats, and unusually cold hooves, ears, and muzzles.

Signs of Toxicity: Thiamin toxicity is very unlikely. Dietary intakes of up to 1,000 times the recommended amount have been safely administered to horses without any ill effects. However, injecting doses of 1,000 to 2,000 mg of thiamin might produce a slowed pulse rate and a mild tranquilizing effect (a result that has been disputed in some research). Certainly thiamin has the reputation, in some circles, of being a tranquilizer (probably due to its action in nerve transmission), but it is important to keep in mind that large doses of this vitamin have produced convulsions, labored breathing, and death by respiratory paralysis in dogs, mice, and rabbits. High doses of thiamin also have been suspected, on occasion, to cause the opposite effect in horses — over-excitation.

RIBOFLAVIN (VITAMIN B₂)

Function: The synthesis of adenosine triphosphate (ATP) depends on riboflavin, as do lipid metabolism and the metabolism of certain drugs. Deficiencies (which have not been documented naturally but have been induced in experimental situations) compromise the tissues most in need of oxygen during strenuous exercise.

Sources: Fresh forage (especially legumes such as alfalfa and clover) and yeast supplements are good sources of riboflavin, a vitamin also synthesized by the gut flora.

Signs of Deficiency: Riboflavin deficiency has not been described in horses, but in other species the signs include decreased feed intake, scaly skin and a dull haircoat, inflammation of the lips and tongue, colon ulcers, and eyes that tear and react painfully to light. Irritation to the eyes also results, with increased tearing, sensitivity to light, and inflammation of the surrounding tissues. Some years ago riboflavin was thought to be involved with periodic ophthalmia (moon blindness); more recent research, however, has absolved it of this responsibility, pointing the finger instead at infection by *Leptospira* or the parasite *Onchocerca cervicalis*.

Signs of Toxicity: Horses tolerate high levels of riboflavin very well, and no signs of toxicity have been documented.

NIACIN (NICOTINIC ACID) AND PANTOTHENIC ACID

Function: Niacin is considered a B vitamin but has no numerical designation. It does share qualities of the other B vitamins, however, being important in the regulation of energy metabolism, especially the processing of carbohydrates, amino acids, and fats. Another B vitamin, pantothenic acid (formerly designated vitamin B_3), also is involved in the metabolism of carbohydrates, fats, and proteins.

Sources: Both pantothenic acid and niacin are widely available in virtually all vegetable matter though some forms may be poorly digestible. Niacin also is produced by microbial fermentation in the horse's cecum.

Signs of Deficiency and Toxicity: Actual niacin or pantothenic acid deficiency — or excess, for that matter — has not been described in horses. Theoretically, because like the other members of the B family, these two vitamins are involved in biochemical reactions in the body, the symptoms of deficiency (if clinically induced) would tend to resemble those described for the other B vitamins.

PYROXIDINE (VITAMIN B₆)

Function: Amino acid metabolism is the main function for pyroxidine, but this vitamin also is involved in glycogen utilization, in the synthesis of epinephrine (adrenaline) and norepinephrine, and in the metabolism of fats.

Signs of Deficiency and Toxicity: Again, no signs of deficiency or excess have actually been documented in the horse because pyroxidine is widely available in the diet and is also manufactured by the intestinal flora. However, in humans, high doses of pyroxidine administered on a daily basis have produced signs of sensory nervous system dysfunctions. Dietary levels of up to 50 times the nutritional requirement are considered safe for horses.

BIOTIN

Function: Most horsepeople are familiar with biotin as a supplement for hooves, but fewer know that it is considered one of the B-complex vitamins. Its primary role is as a co-enzyme in several crucial but complex chemical reactions related to metabolism, including the synthesis of glycerol for body fats, RNA, and DNA. It is considered essential for cell proliferation.

Sources: Biotin is readily available in plant material and manufactured, to a certain level, by the gut microflora. However, researchers debate whether the amount a horse's system produces is adequate for his daily needs. Biotin deficiencies in fish, mink, foxes, pigs, and turkeys have been reported, and, intriguingly, the symptoms that result often include skin, footpad, and/or periople lesions that provide a ready comparison to the thin, shelly hooves some horses grow.

Biotin is a vitamin with which a distinction might be made between the horse's need for it on a nutritional level and the good it might be able to do when administered in much larger amounts. Feeding higher concentrations of biotin makes it, in essence, a pharmaceutical, which has been shown in some cases to improve the quality and speed of hoof horn growth.

Unfortunately, no one has yet established an absolutely optimal level of biotin. The amounts included in most of the popular hoof supplements (from 10 to 30 mg or more) are well above what is considered the base requirement. Fortunately, high levels of biotin are well tolerated, making biotin supplementation a relatively harmless therapy, even if its results vary from horse to horse and might take six to nine months to become obvious.

COBALAMIN (VITAMIN B₁₂) AND FOLACIN FOLIC ACID (FOLATE)

Function: Both of these vitamins are needed for the synthesis of red blood cells, and a deficiency of either will result in anemia. In addition to this role, B_{12} also is required for the production of propionate, a major energy source derived from the fermentation of carbohydrates. Folic acid is required for all sorts of chemical reactions, including DNA synthesis, so it's crucial anytime there's a need for rapid cell growth or replacement. It is also receiving some attention as a potentially beneficial supplement to help combat anemia in high-performance horses.

Sources: While folacin folic acid can be found in green forage, B_{12} is unique among vitamins in that it is synthesized in nature only by micro-organisms. Although the gut flora seem to produce ample B_{12}, the vitamin often is administered to high-performance horses to enhance performance, treat or prevent anemia, and stimulate the appetite. So far, no evidence supports the belief that supplemental B_{12} does any of these things though severely anemic or heavily parasitized horses appear to respond to it. (It should be pointed out that it is likely far more valuable to treat this type of horse through deworming and a proper diet than through B_{12} injections, which only increase plasma concentrations of the vitamin for a short period.)

Signs of Deficiency and Toxicity: Neither has been reported in horses, although horses being treated for equine protozoal myelitis (EPM) can have their folic acid levels compromised by certain drugs.

VITAMIN C (ASCORBIC ACID)

Function: Most of us are familiar with vitamin C but have heard very little of its function or requirement by horses. It is an antioxidant, which protects fats, proteins, and membranes from free radicals. In addition, it enhances the formation of bone and teeth, aids in the utilization of several of the B vitamins as well as cholesterol and glucose, and improves the intestinal absorption of iron. On top of this, it's a component of the connective tissue collagen and several amino acids.

Sources: Humans are one of the few species that because of the lack of a crucial enzyme do not synthesize their own vitamin C from glucose in their livers. For most species, including the horse, vitamin C does not need to be taken in daily from the diet, and, in fact, there is no demonstrated dietary requirement of this vitamin for horses — just as well, as most equines aren't big on citrus fruits.

Signs of Deficiency: The effects of a vitamin C deficiency do not occur in horses though it is suspected that horses over the age of twenty, or those who have been ill or stressed, might sometimes suffer low plasma concentrations of ascorbic acid that could be associated with wound infections, bleeding from the nose, and an increased susceptibility to disease. Some cases of infertility in both mares and stallions also have been reported to improve with the supplementation of vitamin C, but this has yet to be confirmed by research. In any case, oral vitamin C has been shown to be poorly absorbed by the horse, and intramuscular injections of the vitamin tend to cause marked tissue irritation. Intravenous administration has been tried, but the body so efficiently eliminates this water-soluble compound that plasma concentrations only remained elevated for a few hours. The form that is sometimes included in feeds, on the off chance it might have some beneficial effect, is ascorbyl palmitate, which horses (but few other species) can absorb fairly well.

8

CHAPTER

Minerals

O f all the ingredients of a horse's diet, minerals are unique. They make up only the tiniest fraction of the weight of the daily ration, yet they're critically important for literally dozens of daily bodily functions. They contribute no energy and contain no carbon. In fact, essentially, they're rocks — and it can be difficult to imagine their being digested by a horse (or by a human, for that matter).

But without minerals, horses could not metabolize fats, proteins, or carbohydrates; their muscles and nerves would not function normally; and their bones could not support their own weight. Minerals help the blood transport oxygen throughout the body, maintain the body's acid/base and fluid balances, and are necessary components of virtually every enzyme the horse needs for everyday metabolism. They are integral parts of some vitamins, hormones, and amino acids. Yet they make up only about 4% of the horse's total body weight (as compared to 30% to 35% fats, carbohydrates, and proteins, and about 60% water). In the case of minerals, a little bit means a lot.

Minerals are generally divided into two categories: macrominerals, those needed in larger quantities (relatively speaking) in the daily diet, and microminerals, or trace minerals, those needed only in infinitesimal amounts (usually expressed as parts per million, or ppm — or sometimes as the equivalent unit, mg/kg). Macrominerals, which include calcium, phosphorus, magnesium, sodium, potassium, sulfur, and chlorine (as chloride), are described in g/kg, or as percentages. In order to provide some perspective, the micromineral "unit," ppm, is 10,000 times smaller. Iodine, manganese, iron, cobalt, zinc, copper, and selenium are all considered trace minerals necessary to the horse — though the optimum amounts required are, in some cases, still in dispute.

The roles of various minerals in the functioning of the equine body are not always clear cut. Some trace minerals seem to play a role in metabolism, but they have not yet been proven to produce any symptoms of deficiency when not present: These "mystery minerals" include vanadium, tin, silicon, nickel, chromium, molybdenum, fluorine, and arsenic. It's interesting to note that some of these are also minerals that can be categorized as "heavy metals." They are capable of doing significant damage if ingested in large enough amounts. Potentially toxic are lead, arsenic, nickel, aluminum, and cadmium, all heavy metals that might have a tiny role to play in nutrition. Ongoing research will likely reveal more about these ingredients.

All minerals can have adverse effects if present in the diet in large enough amounts, but in most cases there is a broad safety zone. Within that safe range, feeding the minimum amount of a mineral might be just as effective as feeding the maximum amount — and often, considerably less expensive. Of course, the companies that market feed supplements might prefer you believe otherwise!

Making matters even more complicated is the fact that some minerals have "relationships." The amount of one mineral present might affect the absorption and utilization of another. Calcium and phosphorus are the most famous partners. Both are essential to the growth and repair of healthy bone, but they must be present in a certain proportion (with at least as much calcium as phosphorus, never the reverse) to do their jobs. Copper, zinc, and iron (with the possible addition of magnesium and manganese) form another linkage that has received a good deal of scrutiny by researchers exploring developmental bone abnormalities in young horses. And there might be many more connections we don't yet fully understand.

Finally, the absorption of minerals in the horse's gut varies widely. Most of these elements can bind in a number of different molecules, some of which are easier for the horse's digestive system to break down than others. (Zinc, for example, can be found in the diet as zinc carbonate, zinc sulfate, or zinc oxide, to name only three.) The result is that, of the amount of a mineral listed on a product's feed tag, only a very small percentage might actually be used by the horse. For example, the average absorption of calcium varies between 50% and 75% while phosphorus is less well utilized, at about 30% to 55%. Iron absorption is even poorer; less than 15% is typically used. Zinc's range is from 5% all the way up to 90%, up to about 25%, but upward of 100% of ingested sodium is absorbed, especially when sweat losses of this mineral are high.

Feed-company chemists have tried to address the absorption problem in a number of innovative ways, some more successful than others. Organic (plant) sources of minerals often are absorbed better than are the inorganic (artificial) sources feed companies might use to supplement a feed — but even this is not a hard-and-fast rule. For some minerals, absorption can be significantly improved by "chelating" them — a process that bonds minerals to two or more amino acids to form stable biochemical ring compounds, which can be metabolized as much as 300% to 500% more efficiently than their inorganic counterparts. Alas, there is no one magic formula for improving absorption, as what works for one mineral might be a dismal failure with another. This is true even with chelation, which produces very good results with some minerals (including most of the macrominerals) but not all.

Mineral absorption (roughly determined by measuring the amount of the mineral remaining in the manure, compared with the amount contained in the ingested feed) also can be affected by a whole host of other factors. The amount of other nutrients in the diet, such as fats, indigestible fiber, and vitamins, can all have an influence on mineral utilization; so can the pH balance of the gut (which affects the solubility of the minerals).

Nor is the mineral content of feeds etched in stone. It can vary with soil mineral concentrations, plant species, stage of maturity, and conditions at harvesting. All of these factors keep feed industry chemists on their toes as they formulate feeds and supplements for the horse's maximum benefit.

Still, there is much we do understand about the macrominerals and at least some of the trace minerals. Here, then, is a rundown of the most important minerals in your horse's diet. The chemical abbreviations are noted in parantheses.

CALCIUM AND PHOSPHORUS (Ca and P)

Function: First on the feed tag, and in most discussions of minerals, is calcium, a versatile player best known for its role in bone structure and repair. Calcium makes up about 35% of the horse's bone structure, but it also is involved in a host of other functions, including cardiac muscle contraction, cell membrane integrity, glandular secretion, temperature regulation, and blood clotting mechanisms. The absorption efficiency of calcium seems to decline with age and to range from as high as 75% in young horses to 50% or less in older ones.

It is almost impossible to discuss calcium without considering its partner, phosphorus, which is also essential to the growth and maintenance of healthy bones and teeth as well as to energy metabolism and numerous cellular functions. In addition, phosphorus plays an important role in late pregnancy and lactation, during which times a mare's phosphorus needs increase.

The ratio of calcium to phosphorus in the equine diet is crucial. Symptoms of deficiency will result if the horse does not receive at least as much calcium as phosphorus. That 1:1 ratio serves as a baseline, though interestingly, horses can tolerate quite a lot of calcium (more than five times the recommended level) provided the base level of phosphorus is adequate. Most researchers feel the ideal balance is about 1.2 parts calcium to 1 part phosphorus, up to about 1.6:1. Excess dietary phosphorus, in any form, binds calcium and prevents its absorption, but the same is not true in reverse; excess calcium has almost no effect on the absorption of phosphorus.

Signs of Deficiency and Toxicity: Calcium deficiency can have a dramatic effect on skeletal integrity. Symptoms of calcium deficiency can include developmental bone abnormalities in foals, "big head disease" (also called bran disease) in adult horses, decreased bone density, stiffness and possible lameness, weight loss, loose teeth, and fragile bones. Most of the same symptoms will occur if a phosphorus deficiency exists, but excess phosphorus can have a similar effect because it interferes with calcium absorption. Deficiencies of either mineral result in mobilization of these minerals from the bone — that is, they are drawn from the bone matrix and reintroduced to the blood plasma. In this way, while the bone is weakened, the other body functions to which calcium and phosphorus are pivotal are maintained.

Under most circumstances, horses eating forage have a hard time developing a calcium deficiency, as hay (especially legume hay) is calcium-rich. However, a diet very low in forage and high in grains (which are naturally high in phosphorus) can produce these symptoms. Historically, horses fed diets rich in wheat bran often developed this imbalance; today, it's rare. One of the few other causes of calcium deficiency in horses is the ingestion of plants containing high amounts of oxalate compounds, which inhibit calcium absorption. Plants such as sorrel, dock, rhubarb, purslane, kikuyu grass, and lambsquarter can contain potentially harmful amounts of oxalates. They are primarily a problem for young horses and might also cause diarrhea and gastroenteritis.

Although horses can tolerate high levels of calcium, there's now some evidence (extrapolated from other species) that calcium influences gastrin secretion in the stomach. Some researchers believe that unnecessarily high dietary calcium might be implicated in the development of gastric ulcers.

SODIUM AND CHLORIDE (Na and Cl)

Even those for whom chemistry was never a strong subject know that sodium and chloride together make table salt. And the vast majority of horsemen know that salt is a crucial part of the equine diet.

Function: The two elements (Na+ and Cl-) are responsible for the regulation of all the horse's body fluids, as well as the conduction of electrical impulses in nerves and muscles, and are the most important of the minerals known as electrolytes (minerals lost through sweat and urine during exercise stress). Chloride is also an essential ingredient of bile and is important in forming hydrochloric acid, a component of the gastric secretions necessary for digestion.

For maintenance, the horse's diet (as dry matter) should contain at least 0.25% salt (a level that will supply a maintenance level of 0.1% sodium), and if the horse is exercising hard enough to sweat on a regular basis, he should receive 0.75% salt per day. Exact chloride requirements for horses have not been established, but they are thought to be satisfied when the horse ingests enough salt to take care of his sodium requirements. (Salt is not a 50-50 proposition, by the way — chemistry being the complicated thing it is, salt works out to be about 39% sodium and 61% chloride.)

Sources: Many feeds contain less than 0.1% sodium, which is less than needed, even by idle horses. For this reason, horses should always have access to salt in the form of a lick or in loose form. Alternatively, you can add additional salt to your horse's feed, though this is a less perfect solution. Horses have a certain amount of "nutritional wisdom" when it comes to salt and are best left to ingest the amount their bodies tell them they need. (Contrary to popular belief, this nutritional wisdom does not extend to other minerals — horses don't wake up with a craving for cobalt or manganese any more than we do.)

When you provide salt to your horse, you can choose among salt blocks that are iodized, those that have added trace minerals, and those that are just plain salt. While the trace-mineral blocks are a good idea, they still contain mostly salt (about 95% on average) and should not be depended upon to supply all of your horse's other mineral needs. Furthermore, some horses object to the taste of a trace-mineral block and, thus, will not ingest all the salt they require. The best solution might be to provide both plain or iodized salt and a trace-mineral-plus-salt block in your horse's pasture or stall and give him the choice.

It also is worth noting that some horses don't care to use a solid salt block (which, in fairness, is better designed for the tongues of cattle). If your salt block gets ignored, try providing loose salt instead.

Signs of Deficiency: Because horses will usually consume salt in excess of their nutritional needs if it is available, salt deficiencies are almost as rare as real toxicities. However, such losses might occur in stressful situations, such as 100-mile endurance races in very hot, humid conditions. If a sodium chloride deficiency occurs rapidly, muscle contraction and chewing might become uncoordinated, sweating will decrease (with a corresponding decrease in performance), the gait might become unsteady, and plasma concentrations of both sodium and chloride will decrease while potassium will increase. Generally, however, a salt deficiency occurs more slowly and might only be noticeable because the horse begins to lick objects and surfaces that might have salt on them. If salt is not provided, he might become dehydrated and constipated, lose his appetite, and become weakened.

Signs of Toxicity: The absorption levels of sodium and chloride are quite high — from 75% to 95%, by most researchers' estimations. Excesses are readily excreted in the urine, provided the horse has access to fresh, clean water. The only time high salt intake (from adding too much salt to the feed, from drinking brine or sea water out of desperation, or from a salt-block-munching habit) is likely to become a problem occurs when fresh water is restricted. Clinical signs of salt toxicity include colic, diarrhea, frequent urination, paralysis of the hind limbs, staggering and weakness, and eventually, death. It is treated by offering water in small amounts at frequent intervals; too much, too soon might produce cellular swelling and intracranial pressure problems, which can be very dangerous.

POTASSIUM (K)

Function: Potassium, designated by the chemical symbol K, is a crucial element of cellular osmotic pressure and the maintenance of the body's acid/base balance. It is also considered an electrolyte and is usually the other major mineral horsemen are concerned about replacing when a horse is working hard.

Sources: Most forages contain between 1% and 4% potassium, plenty to satisfy the horse's daily requirement of about 0.4% — or even the hard-working horse's requirement of 0.6%. (Even most cereal grains, containing between 0.3% and 0.4% potassium, can usually fulfill the daily requirement without difficulty.)

Those who wish to increase their horse's potassium intake (usually in anticipation of, or in response to, high-stress competition) can do so with a commercial electrolyte product, or by adding 50 to 100 grams of "lite" or "low sodium" salt (half sodium chloride, and half potassium chloride — containing about 26% potassium) to the feed. Lite salt is available in most major supermarkets.

Signs of Deficiency: Without sufficient potassium, horses are prone to fatigue, muscle weakness, exercise intolerance, and decreased water and feed intake. Increased restlessness and spookiness, especially in response to loud noises, have also been reported. Because sweating increases potassium loss, both in the sweat itself and in the urine, temporary deficiencies are a concern particularly for high-level three-day-event and endurance horses, particularly when they are training or competing in hot, humid conditions. Potential potassium losses also can be aggravated by the administration of diuretics such as Lasix/Salix (used to treat racehorses with pulmonary hemorrhages, sometimes called "bleeders"), and are a risk in horses with diarrheal diseases such as Potomac Horse Fever. Outside of these conditions, however, potassium deficiencies are rare.

Signs of Toxicity: Excess potassium intake is not harmful, as it is readily excreted in the urine. The exception is horses suffering from the genetic abnormality HYPP (hyperkalemic periodic paralysis), in which excess potassium tends to build up in the system. The disease, limited to those Quarter Horses, Paints, and Appaloosas descending from the Impressive line, is treated nutritionally by keeping the dietary intake of potassium under 1% (usually by feeding a high-grain, low-forage diet, and avoiding particularly young forage and molasses, which also contains high amounts of the mineral). There are now grain rations with low potassium levels marketed specifically for HYPP horses.

MAGNESIUM (Mg)

Function: About 60% of the body's store of magnesium is tied up in the skeletal structure, and another 30% is found in the muscles, where it plays a role in contracting the muscle fibers. Magnesium is also an important activator of many enzymes.

Sources: The horse's magnesium needs of about 0.1% per day are easily met by a normal diet (the magnesium content of most horse feeds is between 0.1% and 0.3%). Magnesium absorption tends to be in the 40% to 60% range, with utilization of added dietary sources, such as magnesium oxide or magnesium sulfate, sometimes somewhat better (up to about 70%).

Signs of Deficiency and Toxicity: Neither magnesium deficiencies nor toxicities have been reported in horses fed normal diets, except in the rare case of lactating mares that have demonstrated tetany (intermittent muscle spasms, similar to those produced by the disease tetanus) as a possible result of a high-potassium, low-magnesium diet and high levels of magnesium being excreted in the milk.

The condition is far more common in milking cattle, which do not absorb magnesium as efficiently as horses.

Experimentally induced magnesium deficiencies in foals have produced muscle tremors, nervousness, uncoordinated movement, and eventually, collapse, convulsive paddling, and death. There was also, on autopsy, some mineralization (deposits of calcium and phosphorus) in the aorta. There have been few studies on the effects of high-magnesium diets, though horses apparently have a high tolerance for this mineral. The practice of supplementing magnesium for its alleged calming effect, however, does open the door to potential toxicities if administered often. The source of magnesium may be important — in one study, ponies fed high levels of magnesium oxide suffered no ill effects, but horses fed excess magnesium sulfide (which was used prior to the introduction of inhalants and barbiturates, as an intravenous anesthetic) can experience compromised kidney and intestinal function.

SULFUR (S)

Function: We don't tend to think of sulfur as an important mineral, but it is an essential constituent of the amino acids methionine and cysteine, as well as the B vitamins biotin and thiamin and a number of other important molecules such as insulin, heparin (an anti-coagulant) and chondroitin sulfate, a component of cartilage, bone, tendons, and blood vessels. The concentration of sulfur in the body is highest in hooves and hair, which both contain the protein keratin (4% sulfur). Overall, sulfur makes up about 0.15% of the horse's total body weight.

Sources: Despite the mineral's importance, the exact sulfur requirements of the horse have not yet been determined. Most horse feeds contain about 0.15% organic sulfur, which seems to be enough to meet daily requirements. Inorganic sulfur is not readily absorbed by the horse, but organic (bound into amino acids) is.

Signs of Deficiency and Toxicity: Sulfur deficiencies have not been reported in horses, though in other species it causes decreased appetite, growth, and milk production. In pigs and ruminants, excess dietary sulfur interferes with copper absorption, but so far there is no evidence that this occurs in horses. In fact, no side effects have been noted from high sulfur intake in equines, as the mineral is easily excreted in the urine and feces.

TRACE MINERALS

SELENIUM (Se)

Function: Although it is needed in infinitesimal amounts, selenium is a mineral that has received a lot of press in recent years. Selenium and vitamin E function in a partnership that helps protect body tissues from free-radical damage that occurs during oxidation (the conversion of foodstuff into energy). In particular, they act as a defense mechanism against damage to cell membranes and enzymes. While vitamin E blocks free radical attacks on lipids, selenium is a component of the enzyme glutathione peroxidase, which helps prevent the formation of free radicals and destroys lipo- and hydrogen peroxidases that are released into the cells. This dynamic duo works best when both minerals are present in the correct amounts.

Selenium also plays a role in the control of thyroid hormone metabolism.

Signs of Toxicity: Selenium is a tricky mineral for several reasons. First, unlike most minerals that have a broad safety range, selenium has a very low threshold of toxicity for horses — only a few parts per million beyond the recommended levels. (Most other livestock species have a much higher tolerance, partly because their absorption rates are lower than horses'.) Thus, the assumption that "if some is good, more is better" is a particularly dangerous one for this mineral — and the effects of selenium toxicity can be worse than the effects of a deficiency. They can include patchy sweating, blind staggers, colic, diarrhea, and increased heart and respiration rates if acute (as in, for example, when a horse is given selenium injections). Chronic toxicity can cause hair loss, especially in the mane and tail, the cracking of hooves around the coronary band, and occasionally hooves that, shockingly, slough off completely.

That said, a survey of veterinary and laboratory reports up to 1993, revealed reports of selenium-deficiency disease in livestock (including horses) in 46 of the 50 states The selenium content of feeds can vary — depending on where the plants were grown — and across North America, the soil content of selenium fluctuates significantly. Some areas are so selenium-deficient that crops grown there are considered to contain no selenium at all, necessitating supplementation. Some locations have adequate selenium in the soil, and others actually have toxic concentrations of selenium, making any supplementation positively reckless. Pockets where toxic levels exist are In California, Colorado, Idaho, Montana, Oregon, South Dakota, Utah, and Wyoming; however, all of these states except Wyoming also report areas that are deficient. The Great Lakes region, and almost all of Canada except for southern Manitoba, Saskatchewan, and Alberta, tend to be severely selenium-deficient.

This extreme variation from region to region is the reason that regulations exist in Canada and in most of the United States to make sure feed companies print a warning to consumers if selenium has been added to a feed. What might be appropriate to feed in one region would be a very poor choice in another.

Because the toxicity threshold of selenium is so low (between 2 and 5 ppm), you should be aware of the selenium content of your local soils (and, thus, your pasture and your hay) before you choose a vitamin-E-and-selenium supplement or a selenium-added feed for your horse. Even some trace-mineral salt blocks contain added selenium, so be sure to check the label before you place it in the pasture. Information on the selenium content of your local soils can be obtained from your local agriculture extension specialist, or even your local feed store or co-op.

The level of selenium currently recommended for horses is between 0.1 ppm and 0.3 ppm (dry matter). In recent studies, 0.1

mg/kg was sufficient to prevent signs of deficiency, though it's possible that slightly more selenium is necessary for optimum immune function.

Signs of Deficiency: In mild selenium deficiencies, the only symptom might be an increased susceptibility to disease, due to a depressed immune system, and/or decreased fertility in breeding stock. Far less common are severe selenium deficiencies, which are characterized by weakness, impaired movement, difficulty in swallowing, impaired cardiac function, and respiratory distress. Selenium deficiencies have also been implicated in certain types of "tying up" in performance horses. Young foals, from birth to about four weeks old, are most likely to demonstrate clinical symptoms (which occur as a result of inadequate selenium intake by the dam during pregnancy). They might develop muscle pain, an inability to nurse, and a stilted hopping gait in the rear legs, or be stillborn or die within a few days after birth. This is sometimes referred to as "white muscle disease." In areas where selenium deficiency is a documented problem in foals, the dam should receive supplementation throughout her pregnancy, and the foal given a vitamin-E-and-selenium injection just after birth.

IODINE (I)

Function: Iodine is a specialist. It is essential for the synthesis of thyroid hormones thyroxin (T4) and tri-iodothyronine (T3), which help regulate basal metabolism. Unlike some other minerals, which fulfill numerous functions, this is iodine's only known role in the diet.

The horse's estimated daily requirement of iodine is 0.1 ppm (or 1-3 mg per 500 kg horse per day, depending on the level of work done), and like selenium (and unlike practically every other mineral), iodine's toxicity threshold is quite low, about 5 ppm (40 mg/horse/day).

Sources: Most horse feeds contain between 0.05 and 0.2 ppm (dry matter) of iodine, but some might contain as much as 2 ppm, depending on the soils in which the feed was grown. Thus, it is possible for horses to become iodine deficient on a normal diet, though feeding an iodized or trace-mineral salt (at a level of as little as half an ounce a day) can easily prevent deficiencies. It also is possible for horses to ingest toxic amounts of iodine, either as a result of over-supplementing with iodized salt (if it is more than 4% of the total diet), or by feeding seaweed (kelp) or supplements containing it, on top of a feed already enriched with iodine. Seaweed might contain as much as 1,850 ppm of iodine — and at that level, as little as 0.7 ounces a day might be harmful. Pregnant and lactating mares seem to be less tolerant of high levels of iodine than other horses. Overall, in recent years, reports of iodine toxicosis have been more frequent than reports of deficiencies. Some researchers have chalked this up to overzealous supplementing by well-meaning owners.

Signs of Deficiency and Toxicity. Both iodine deficiencies and excesses produce very similar symptoms   they both result in a goiter, a swelling of the thyroid gland on the underside of the horse's throat, just under the jaw. This can make it rather difficult to discern at first glance whether you are dealing with too much or too little iodine. The best way to determine the problem is to evaluate the iodine levels in the diet, as blood plasma levels of thyroid hormones can fluctuate quite a lot. If no seaweed or supplemental sources of iodine are being fed, then chances are you are dealing with a deficiency.

Other symptoms of an iodine imbalance are a dry, lusterless hair-coat; hair loss; decreased growth and decreased bone calcification in young horses; lethargy and drowsiness; and cold intolerance and possible hypothermia (low body temperature). Sometimes an iodine deficiency (but not an excess) will produce a thickened skin due to the accumulation of mucinous material under the skin of the limbs. This is called myxedema.

Iodine-deficient mares may have abnormal estrous cycles, and their foals are often stillborn or born weak.

As with many mineral imbalances, detrimental effects of too much or too little iodine are most obvious in foals. Severely affected foals (usually born to mares with iodine imbalances) are weak, have difficulty standing, suffer persistent hypothermia (with an abnormally low rectal temperature of less than 100 degrees Celsius), and have a weak sucking response. They might suffer respiratory distress as well and have noticeably enlarged thyroids. Most die within a few days of birth. Those who survive might suffer from various bone and joint abnormalities. Iodine toxicosis might also increase a horse's susceptibility to infectious diseases.

COPPER (Cu)

Function: This mineral is a component of several enzymes involved in the synthesis and maintenance of elastic connective tissue, the mobilization of iron stores, and synthesis of the body pigment melanin, as well as being involved in the health and preservation of cellular mitochondria.

The liver regulates copper metabolism by storing it or excreting it in the bile. Its absorption in the gut might be influenced by the levels of other minerals, such as zinc, iron, sulfur, selenium, cadmium, and molybdenum, making it somewhat difficult to estimate how much dietary copper is utilized. Because copper toxicity only occurs at relatively high levels in horses (in contrast to some other species — sheep in particular are very sensitive to it), most feed companies err on the side of generosity when it comes to copper, in the hopes that enough will be absorbed to meet the horse's needs. The exact optimum levels of copper in the equine diet have not yet been established. The National Research Council recommends a level of 10 mg/kg of ration, which many researchers feel is low. (Some have suggested a level of 50 mg/kg for creep-feeding foals, and at least 25 mg/kg for weanlings up to twelve months old. Despite a number of studies, however, since the NRC's 1989 recommendation was released, there is still a shortage of data on copper requirements of adult, exercising horses indicating that level should be re-evaluated.

Signs of Deficiency: Copper deficiencies might play a role in developmental orthopedic diseases of young horses (though some researchers now believe its participation might have been over-rated), and the deficiencies also have been implicated in ruptures of the aorta or uterine arteries in aged foaling mares.

Real copper deficiencies have rarely been noted in horses. A foal getting inadequate amounts of copper might have abnormal bone or cartilage development but will not suffer slowed growth. And because copper absorption decreases when copper intake increases, symptoms of copper excess only have been noted in horses in exper-imental situations when very high levels have been fed.

IRON (Fe)

Function: Most of us are familiar with iron's role in hemoglo-bin, the molecule that enables red blood cells to transport oxygen throughout the body. Approximately 60% of the body's iron is involved in this task, with another 40% incorporated in muscle myoglobin, storage forms, and various enzymes.

Sources: The horse's estimated iron needs are about 50 ppm per day for pregnancy, lactation, and growth, and 40 ppm for other mature equines. Most forages contain between 50 and 250 ppm (occasionally, up to 400 ppm) of iron, so under most conditions horses receive plenty of iron in their normal diets.

Signs of Deficiency: Despite a low absorption rate (estimated at 15% or less), clinically recognized iron deficiencies rarely occur in either foals or mature horses at any performance level. Only under conditions of severe or chronic blood loss is an iron deficiency like-ly. Sometimes this blood loss is not obvious (it might be the result of a severe intestinal parasite problem or even a serious case of lice).

If a deficiency does occur, the horse will exhibit impaired per-formance, followed by anemia (low red blood cell count). Because iron levels are tied to fitness, iron supplements have a reputation for enhancing athletic performance, but they should never be adminis-tered unless a blood test has demonstrated actual anemia.

Signs of Toxicity: Iron toxicosis is far more common in horses than an iron deficiency. Foals are particularly susceptible to iron excesses in the first few days of their lives. Excess iron is stored in various tissues, especially the liver, and severely affected foals (who have usually received inappropriate doses of iron) might suffer depression, dehydration, diarrhea, liver failure, and death. It's important to note that the body has no way to excrete excess iron; its only means of protection is decreased absorption, which works with oral supplements but not with injectables.

High levels of iron depress the absorption of other minerals, such as zinc and copper, and also might make horses more vulnerable to bacterial infections. (Bacteria will multiply more efficiently when it is readily available.) Corticosteroids are a source of iron, which is one reason why these drugs might increase a horse's susceptibility to bacterial infections.

ZINC (Zn)

Function: The metabolism of proteins and carbohydrates is assisted by more than 100 enzymes containing zinc. The absorption of this mineral is affected by the level of many other minerals, including copper and iron, but remains low, averaging only 5% to 15% digestibility. Forty ppm of zinc per day has been recommended for adult horses, and a higher level might be beneficial for foals (zinc is considered to play a role in growth and prevention of developmental orthopedic disorders, but to what extent no one is yet sure).

Signs of Deficiency and Toxicity: Horses are quite tolerant of high levels of zinc. Zinc toxicosis, resulting from horses grazing in pastures contaminated by zinc smelters or mines, brass foundries, or other industrial plants, has been noted (with symptoms including bony limb deformities, growth plate enlargements, and in severely affected foals, lameness and a strange low-headed, arched-back stance), but it does not occur under normal conditions. Likewise, clinical symptoms of zinc deficiency have only been produced experimentally (foals fed a zinc-deficient diet had reduced appetite and growth rates, accompanied by hair loss). The average level of dietary zinc in most feedstuff, about 15 ppm, would appear to be inadequate (and is often supplemented by feed companies).

MANGANESE (Mn)

Function: Lipid and carbohydrate metabolism depends on manganese, and this mineral is also essential for the synthesis of the chondroitin sulfate needed for cartilage formation. These are functions involved mostly in reproduction and growth. The exact amount of manganese needed by horses is still under debate, but 40 ppm per day is generally considered ample.

Signs of Deficiency and Toxicity: Although manganese deficiencies are sometimes problems in ruminants, they have not been described in horses. Such a deficiency would likely result in fertility problems in adult breeding stock and in limb deformities in foals.

There is more good news: Manganese is among the least toxic of the trace elements, and there are no known instances of manganese toxicity in horses. Large doses of this mineral might, however, interfere with phosphorus absorption.

COBALT (Co)

Function: Cobalt's only known function is as a component of vitamin B_{12} — so a cobalt deficiency results in a B_{12} deficiency. Based on levels recommended for cattle, a minimum of 0.05 mg/kg of cobalt, and a maximum of 10 mg/kg, is suggested for horses, but neither deficiencies nor excesses of this mineral (nor of vitamin B_{12}) have been described in horses as yet. Most researchers suspect that neither is likely to occur.

CHROMIUM (Cr)

This little-known trace mineral plays a role in carbohydrate and lipid metabolism, helps insulin process glucose and may be important for horses with glucose intolerance/insulin resistance issues (more on this in Chapter 11). In humans and cattle, chromium supplementation increased the availability of blood glucose to muscles, helped prevent large peaks in insulin activity, and provided a boost to the immune system as well. Unfortunately, very little work has been done to date regarding chromium requirements in horses. Preliminary studies of chromium-supplemented exercising horses did show that they metabolized glucose at a faster rate and had lower levels of cortisol (a hormone produced when horses are stressed), suggesting that horses with high energy demands might benefit from extra chromium — but they also resulted in higher than usual heart rates and blood lactate levels. So while chromium supplementation enjoys some popularity as a treatment for recurrent exertional rhabdomyolysis (RER, or "tying up") and as a calming agent, neither use really can be sanctioned until more definitive studies have been done.

Calcium and Phosphorus Needed by the Horse as Compared to Amount in Common Feeds

	Calcium (% in total diet dry matter)	Phosphorus (% in total diet dry matter)
Amount recommended for:		
Adult maintenance	0.3	0.2
Pregnancy and lactation	0.5	0.3
Growth: 1-4 months	0.8	0.5
Growth: 6-12 months	0.7	0.4
Growth: 12-10 months	0.5	0.3
Growth: 18 months - mature	0.4	0.25
Amount present in:		
Grains	0.05–0.09	0.3–0.4
Wheat Bran	0.1	1.3
Grass Hay	0.3–0.5	0.1–0.3
Legume Hay	0.8–2.0	0.1–0.3

From Lon D. Lewis' *Feeding and Care of the Horse* (1996),
2nd ed. (Page 22, Table 2-2)

Hay and Forage

Now that we've discussed at great length the basic components of the equine diet, let's look at how we can use various foodstuff to provide an ideal nutritional balance.

We've said it before; we'll say it again: Forage should be the basis of any equine diet. So understanding pasture, hay, and other fiber sources — how they're grown, harvested, stored, plus how to recognize quality — is an important part of your everyday management. So, too, is knowing which fiber sources are appropriate for your horse.

Forage can be loosely defined as any feed made up of the stems, leaves, and stalks of plants, and which has a minimum fiber content of 18% and a relatively low dietary energy (DE) content. The most natural, least expensive, and safest feed for horses, forage provides the bulk of nutrients horses require for their everyday maintenance metabolism and stimulates the muscle tone and the activity of the gastrointestinal tract. Horses with inadequate amounts of forage in their diets run the risk of colic and founder, as well as stable vices derived from having too little to chew on.

Although horses have been known to nibble on tree leaves and branches, they're primarily grazers, not browsers like deer, and grasses make up most of their natural diet. If you live in a temperate climate with no chance of drought, your horses might have the luxury of nutritious grazing — fresh forage — year-round. But for most North Americans, there's a good portion of the year when good pasture is just not available, and hay — grasses and/or legumes that have been sun cured, dried, and baled for convenient feeding — picks up the slack.

Hay, the most common type of forage fed to horses, averages 28% to 38% crude fiber and has a DE level of about 1.95 to 2.5 Mcal per kg. (Cereal grains, by contrast, contain between 2% and 12% crude fiber and have a much higher DE, averaging 3.3% to 3.7% Mcal/kg.) Hay is high in calcium

and low in phosphorus — and happily, grains are generally high in phosphorus and low in calcium, so a horse being fed both hay and grain usually ingests a Ca:P ratio that "balances out." Hay also contains high levels of potassium and vitamins A, E, and K — and if sun cured, high levels of vitamin D as well. (Vitamins tend to break down over time, so the more recently the hay was cut, the higher the vitamin content; by the time baled hay is a year old, it may contain no appreciable amount of vitamin A.)

Hay can be extremely variable in protein content. Legume hays (such as alfalfa or clover) might contain 20% crude protein or even higher while grass hays (such as timothy, Bermuda grass, or orchard grass) average about 11% to 14% protein and can go as low as 4%. The protein content of hay is largely determined when it is cut — the younger the hay, the higher the protein. Hay cut past the mid-bloom stage (when about 50% of the plants have flowered and gone to seed) is a good deal lower in protein content, and mature (full-bloom or past-bloom) hay might be inadequate to meet an adult horse's nutrient requirements.

There are actually three types of hay, but one type, cereal grain hay, is rarely fed to horses in North America as it is not terribly economical. Cereal grain hay is hay cut from grains such as wheat or barley while the plant is still green and before the seed is harvested.

It is nutritionally similar to grass hay, and the more grain (seeds) the hay contains, the higher its nutritional value. (If the seed heads are lost in harvesting, only straw remains; it makes good bedding but poor feed.)

Far more common are grass hays and legume hays. Of the legumes, alfalfa, also called lucerne, is the most popular crop; it's estimated that more than half of the hay harvested in the United States is alfalfa, or an alfalfa/grass mix. Other legume hay includes clovers (varieties include red, crimson, and ladino, and alsike), birdsfoot trefoil, lespedeza, cowpeas, vetch, and even soybeans. Horses almost always prefer legume hays over grass hays, and this type contains two to three times the protein and calcium of grasses, as well as more soluble (non-fibrous) carbohydrates, beta-carotene (the precursor of vitamin A), and vitamin E. Because of these qualities, they're the preferred hays for young, growing horses as well as lactating mares. But legumes are generally more costly, and in some parts of North America might be infested with poisonous blister beetles.

There are also a number of different types of grass hay, with timothy being the most widely grown across North America; it's an easy crop to establish on most soils, and tolerates cold well, beginning to grow actively early in the spring, weeks before most other hay crops. But timothy doesn't cope well with extremes of heat and humidity, so in the central and southern United States, growers may turn to alternatives such as quick-curing Coastal Bermuda grass (a variety developed to grow tall enough to harvest as hay, unlike its cousin, common Bermuda, which suits better as a lawn), brome (drought resistant and hardy, and also cold tolerant, but less palatable than some other grasses, and so usually grown in combination with alfalfa) or orchard grass (a very drought-resistant species that can be productive even on poor soils). Bluegrass, fescue, reed canarygrass, ryegrass, and Sudan grass are some of the other varieties of grass hays fed to horses. Not only do grass hays not harbor blister beetles, but they often are less dusty than legume hays, making them a preferred choice for horses with respiratory problems. And their more modest protein content makes them a better choice than legumes for mature horses not being used for breeding.

You can distinguish a grass hay from a legume by looking at the stalks and leaves: Grass hays grow tall, upright stalks and long, slender leaves that sheathe the stalk itself, rather than branching out on stems the way legume leaves do. Legume stalks are often coarser, and the leaves are less firmly attached — which leads to increased wastage after harvest, when the dry leaves tend to shatter and crumble out of the bale. The seed heads of grass hays, however, can vary a great deal, from the narrow, cattail-like structures of timothy, to the branched, tree like fronds of bluegrass and orchard grass and the elaborate tufts of brome. Some grasses create a thick, underlying carpet of roots and connecting runners called rhizomes, which protect the ground from water runoff and traffic damage; this makes them a preferred crop for pastures.

There are considerable advantages to growing grass and legume hays together as one crop. First, horses consider legumes tops in the palatability sweepstakes, so combining the two might encourage a horse that would turn his nose up at straight grass hay to accept and consume a mixed "flake." Second, a lower-protein grass hay might help "balance out" the high protein level of a legume and create bales that are appropriate to feed to mature horses — and more marketable for the farmer. And third, the addition of nitrogen-producing legumes to a grass hay crop actually helps fertilize the field and increase the yield of the grass hay. In many parts of North American, "mixed" hay is the preferred feed for horses — though the mix may be any of a number of combinations of legumes and grasses, depending on the climate, soil type, and demand.

Harvesting and Storing

The standard method of harvesting hay is to cut the crop and allow it to sun cure until it has a moisture content of less than 20%, after which it is baled. Growers have to do a delicate dance with the weather, cutting their hay when they hope there is the greatest likelihood of the crop's drying before it is rained on. Sometimes they lose the gamble. The stage of growth of the hay limits the weather window considerably; to ensure good nutritional content, hay should be cut before it reaches the mid-bloom stage. Once seed heads have formed, the plant puts its energy into propagation, and the stalk and leaves become tougher, more fibrous, and less palatable. The crude protein level of brome grass, for example, might drop from 12.6% (mid-bloom) to 5.6% when fully mature. (Researchers have estimated that allowing hay plants to stand past the "boot" stage, when seed heads first appear, decreases crude protein levels by about 0.25% per day, and digestible energy by nearly 0.50% per day.)

Moisture levels are crucial to hay quality. An ill-timed thunderstorm while hay is curing can reduce the leaf content in the resulting bales by up to 15%, destroy up to 34% of the nonstructural carbohydrates as well as 25% of the protein yield, and decrease the overall yield of the crop by up to 40%. Baling while the moisture of the hay is still too high (over 20%, or 18% for large rectangular or round bales) increases the chance of mold growth, decreases the protein utilization, and makes the hay less palatable. In addition, hay that is baled wet tends to generate heat (both through the continued respiration of the hay, which can create an environment of 90% to 100% humidity in the bale, and the metabolic activity of microorganisms associated with the plant material — including heat-resistant fungi that become active at a temperature between 113 and 150 degrees Fahrenheit). Once these processes are set in motion in baled hay, temperatures can continue to rise for about four to 10 weeks (especially when stored in a warm loft with poor air circulation), and at temperatures above 175 degrees F, heat-producing chemical reactions serve to worsen the situation further. A subsequent rapid oxidation of reactive compounds in the hay actually can cause the temperature to rise to ignition point — between 448 and 527 degrees F — and if enough oxygen is present, spontaneous combustion might result, not only destroying the hay, but putting horses and buildings at huge risk.

Bales that feel or smell warm should never be stored anywhere near a barn, and regular checks with a thermometer (slipped down between bales in your stack) are an excellent safety precaution. Hay that heats above 140 degrees F should be removed from the barn — slowly, as even throwing or moving the hay quickly could be enough to cause it to burst into flames. Though regular "square" bales of hay can vary from about 40 to 100 pounds, any unusually heavy bales should be regarded as suspicious — they might have too high a moisture content and are better discarded.

It is best to sun-cure hay until the moisture content is less than 20%.

Heating occurs, to some extent, in all forage materials that contain more than 15% moisture, and many farmers use spray-on drying agents (often containing potassium carbonate), to reduce the risk of baling too wet. The chemicals in the drying agents break down the waxy cuticle layer on the stem, which increases the rate of moisture loss and can cut curing time by 50% to 70%. They also make the leaves less brittle, which results in less leaf (and nutrient) loss.

Another approach is to use a hay preservative, such as propionic acid, which inhibits mold and can allow growers to bale hay at up to 25% moisture. The resulting hay tends to have higher yields, better color, a higher percentage of leaves, and less dust and mildew than conventionally baled hay — not a bad payoff for a chemical that costs about $5 per ton of hay. Both hay preservatives and drying agents have been demonstrated to be safe for use on hay for horses and have no demonstrated effect on palatability. Their only drawback is that some of the chemicals are corrosive to the growers' equipment. Growers producing large square or round bales often use these products as a precaution against spoilage even when curing conditions are ideal.

Check hay for excessive heat.

Even under the best conditions, hay suffers losses of about 30% to 70% during the harvesting and baling processes, with legumes taking a higher toll than the tougher grasses. Losses from normal respiration account for about 5% or 6% of the total dry matter (and that number can rise if the humidity is high). Another 10% to 25% can be lost in raking and baling. Legume leaves, in particular, can shatter and fall to the ground as they dry, and high leaf loss can significantly compromise the nutritional value and, therefore, the quality, of the hay. The leaves of a legume contain about two-thirds of the digestible energy, three-quarters of the protein, and most of the other nutrients.

In warmer regions of North America, growers sometimes are able to get as many as seven or eight cuttings from a hayfield, although in the northern states and Canada two (or at most three) cuttings are the norm. "First cut" hay is generally high in nutritional value if harvested at the proper time and runs the lowest risk of blister beetles (which usually appear after midsummer). Sometimes it contains large numbers of weeds that have grown up since the last cutting of the previous season, and because it is harvested early in the year, it might be more difficult to get it sun cured without its being rained on. Later cuttings, in the heat of the summer, have lower nutritional value because when temperatures are hot, the plants put their energy into rapid growth, with more stem and fewer leaves. But as the weather gets cooler in the fall, hay cuttings usually have a higher leaf and nutrient content, fewer weeds, and, in many areas, the best opportunity of being harvested without rain. Determining the quality of your hay should be based less on which "cut" it is from and more on stage of bloom when harvested.

Assessing Quality

Much of the assessment of the quality of your hay can be done the old-fashioned way: Break open a bale and scratch n' sniff! Good quality hay should be green rather than yellow or brown. (Keep in mind that some hays, particularly some varieties of clover, can cure to quite a dark color, and that this is not necessarily an indicator of mold growth.) It should have a high leaf content ("stemmy" hay is too mature) and few weeds; it should also smell pleasant and slightly sweet. There should be no visible mold (white or dark, matted patches in the hay) or other foreign material. Taking a handful of hay and squeezing it should not hurt your hand — prickly hay has been cut too late and has a low nutrient content. And if you drop a flake of hay from a height of a few feet, you should not see clouds of dust rising from it — dust is usually an indicator that the grower had the tines on his harvester set too low. As a general rule, the nicer you feel that the loose hay would be to sleep in, the better the quality!

To really determine the nutrient content of the hay, however, you'll need to do a hay analysis, as mentioned in Chapter 4. Appearance is a poor indicator of nutritive value — even grass hays that appear very similar can vary in protein content by two to three times. Performing a hay analysis whenever you receive a shipment of hay is an excellent routine to establish, especially as the results may have a significant impact on the grains and supplements you choose to feed.

How much to feed? As a rough guideline, horses should consume 1% to 2% of their bodyweight each day in forage products

— at least 50% of their total diets under all but the most extreme exercise programs. Though all of us prefer to feed by "eyeballing" amounts, the weight and size of a flake of hay can vary so much that it is worth weighing the flakes to determine how close you are to these guidelines. This can be done very simply by standing on a bathroom scale, with and without the flake of hay, and subtracting the difference.

When feeding hay, remember that, at heart, horses are grazing animals, programmed to chew on stemmy, fibrous plants for at least 12 hours a day. That urge to chew can be almost as compelling as a rodent's, so hay fulfills two functions in your barn: It provides nutrients (and keeps the digestive system in good health), but it also keeps horses busy (and thus not chewing the wood fences, stall doors, or their neighbors' tails!). An almost constant supply of small amounts of hay is far more beneficial than one or two large feedings a day because it mimics the horse's natural grazing habits. Make lots of good-quality hay the basis of your horses' diets, and you'll reap the benefits in terms of both health and contentment.

A Few Alternatives

Though regular baled hay is the mainstay of equine diets across North America, it's not the only forage option. Hay also can be pressed into cubes, chopped and processed into pellets, or fermented as silage or "haylage." If your horse suffers from chronic respiratory allergies (such as chronic obstructive pulmonary disease, also called "broken wind" or "heaves"), has dental troubles that make chewing hay difficult, or is very elderly, one of these alternative forms of forage might be just the ticket.

Hay cubes and pellets are simply hay that has been chopped coarsely or finely and formed (with the addition of a binder) into scoopable, baggable pieces. They're more convenient to move around than baled hay and have the advantage of a guaranteed nutritional content, posted on the bag — so you'll know exactly what you're delivering in terms of nutrients. Hay cubes and pellets come in a variety of sizes and textures, from soft and crumbly to quite hard, and they might be all-alfalfa, all-grass hay, a mixture of the two, or even hay mixed with other products such as ground corn cobs. Horses generally prefer hard, crunchy products, but if you are feeding a toothless octogenarian, for example, you can easily soak hay cubes or pellets in a bit of water to make them easier to consume. Soaked or unsoaked, these processed hay products have a significant advantage over regular hay for an allergic horse: They are many times less dusty than even the highest-quality baled forage (even

Pellets are an alternative to hay.

so, be sure to sort out the small particles in the bottom of the bag). Some horses with chronic heaves can become almost symptomless when, along with other management changes to minimize dust, hay is eliminated from the diet in favor of hay cubes or pellets.

The downside of processed hay products? There are really only three. The first is that, unlike a hay bale you can crack open and examine, assessing the quality of the forage used to make the product can be difficult. Despite the guaranteed analysis on the feed tag, it's impossible to tell whether weeds, dirt, or other contaminants have been incorporated into the cubes or pellets. The best advice is to buy from a reputable company and look for pieces of a uniform color and texture with a pleasant smell. This brings us to the second disadvantage of processed hay products: They are usually considerably more expensive than ordinary hay. However, it's very true in the feed business that you get what you pay for, so pass over the most inexpensive hay cube or pellet you see in favor of a better-quality feed that likely will have a higher price tag. The difference will be worth it in terms of peace of mind.

Finally, the convenient shape of hay cubes or pellets can in itself be a disadvantage. Because they take less time to chew than regular hay, horses generally consume them faster — and might be left with a dissatisfied chewing urge. Be prepared for the possibility of boredom-based destructive behaviors as a result.

The other alternative form of hay is usually called haylage, or, sometimes, "horsehage." This is hay harvested at its nutritive best, then stored in anaerobic conditions while still at a relatively high moisture content. It is often treated as a dry silage — that is, the hay is baled as usual (often in large round bales) and then coated in heavy plastic to encourage fermentation. If properly done, ensiling ensures that the hay retains its nutrients much better than it would have if sun cured; it maintains high levels of protein, carbohydrates, carotene, and many vitamins better than any other method of feed preservation. (Because haylage is not exposed to the sun, however, it is lower in vitamin D than naturally cured hay.)

When anaerobic conditions are maintained correctly while making haylage, molds, yeasts, and aerobic bacteria perish while anaerobic microorganisms present in the hay ferment the soluble carbohydrates, producing lactic and volatile fatty acids. In fact, the process mimics what happens in the horse's own cecum and colon when forage is digested. The acids inhibit microbial growth, eventually stopping the fermentation after several weeks. The moisture content of the feed must be monitored carefully, as too high or too low a level might allow excess heat to be generated (which results in spoilage), or the growth of yeasts, molds, and toxic bacteria.

Good haylage should have a clean, pleasant acidic odor; be uniform in color, green to brownish; and feel moist but not mushy or slimy. Dark brown, caramelized, or charred-looking or -smelling feed is a sign that excessive heating occurred during fermentation, and black patches indicate rot. Haylage like this should obviously not be fed. Likewise, anything with an unpleasant or sharp odor should be tossed out. Healthy haylage should have a pH of 3.5 to 5.0 (this can easily be tested with a pH strip). Botulism, a potentially toxic anaerobic bacterium, is a particular risk with haylage. It can brew in any bale with a pH over 4.5. Because the plastic covering protects the haylage from microbial growth, any feed in plastic that has been ripped or punctured should be discarded. Once you do open a package, feed the haylage within a couple of days at maximum.

Despite the greater care required, many horsepeople prefer haylage to traditional sun-cured bales, citing its extremely good palatability (most horses, once familiar with it, strongly prefer it to regular hay), its superior nutritive value, its almost dust-free qualities (making it another good choice for a horse with COPD), and the lack of wastage. Because its moisture content is higher than that of hay, however, it may take two to three times as much haylage to replace each flake of hay.

Next, we'll have a look at the many types of grains available.

Hay Nutrient Content for Horses

Hay Type	DE (Mcal/ kg)	Crude Protein (%)	Crude Fiber (%)	Calcium (%)	Phosphorus (%)	Vitamin A (IU/kg x 1000)	Vitamin E (mg/kg)
Legume—early bloom	2.4	17–20	21–30	1.0–1.8	0.1–0.3	50–85	20–40
Legume—full bloom	2.1	15–18	32	1.0–1.9	0.1–0.3	10–30	10–20
Grass—early bloom	2.1	11–14	30–34	0.3–0.5	0.1–0.3	15–25	10–30
Grass— mature	1.8	6–10	32–36	0.3–0.5	0.1–0.3	5–15	
Cereal grains, cut green	1.9	9	29	0.15–0.35	0.1–0.3	10–35	

From Lon D. Lewis, *Feeding and Care of the Horse* (1996),
2nd ed. (Page 64, Table 4-1)

Grains

I t's five p.m., and up and down the aisle of a large boarding stable, the nickering, rumbling, and pawing begin. What's the cause of the excitement? Nothing more than a metal scoop digging into a bin of grain, a sound that tips off every equine resident that it's dinnertime. Hay seldom receives this sort of reception; it's grain that horses really relish.

But just because horses love grain doesn't mean it's an essential part of their diet. In a wild state, they encounter grain only as an occasional plant seedhead — certainly never in the volumes found in their feed buckets in a domestic scenario. While their teeth can grind grain seeds quite efficiently, their digestive systems are poorly equipped to deal with the low-fiber, high-carbohydrate wallop that grain delivers, thus the much higher incidence of colic among grain-fed horses compared with those fed only forages.

As most of us know, the intake of an excess quantity of any type of grain can result in dire consequences, including life-threatening colic and founder. Unfortunately, equines have no dietary wisdom when it comes to grain, and given the opportunity to gorge themselves (if for instance, the feed room door is left open), they can conceivably eat themselves to death. Because of this, grain should never be fed free-choice or left so that it is accessible to horses outside of their allotted amount at mealtimes. And except in some very exceptional circumstances (largely, horses in hard race training), the grain portion should never be more than 50%, by weight, of a horse's total daily ration. It need not be fed at all, in fact, unless you wish to supplement the energy or nutrient demands of your horses beyond what their forage provides. A good many pleasure horses, especially those that are "easy keepers," do very nicely without the addition of grain to their diets.

Grains in their natural state supply very little in the way of vitamins (commercially mixed rations are generally vitamin-supplemented), but they do

provide an important mineral that might be lacking in a horse on a forage-only diet: phosphorus. Hay and pasture provide generous amounts of the macromineral calcium, but an inadequate amount of phosphorus. Both of these minerals are crucial to correct bone and muscle development and maintenance, and the ratio between them in the horse's diet is pivotal (as we saw in Chapter 8). Too little phosphorus, and bone-building and repair are not carried out as they should be; too much, and the whole system is out of balance and seeks to re-establish it by leaching existing calcium out of the bone, eventually causing bone abnormalities. So grains, which are generally high in phosphorus and low in calcium, can make the perfect companion to hay because when both are fed in the correct quantities, they provide an almost ideal Ca:P ratio for the horse.

An individual grain is actually the seedhead of the plant, containing the nutrient store for the germ (embryo) from which a new plant develops. It consists of a coat, a starchy endosperm, and the germ itself. Some grains, such as barley, rice, oats, and husked sorghum (milo) have a fused husk or hull, which provides extra fiber; others, such as corn, wheat, rye, and millet, do not.

The grains that are fed to horses vary greatly from continent to continent. In North America and parts of Europe, oats and corn are the most popular, but milo (sorghum) is commonly fed to all types of livestock in Central America, and wheat (despite its low palatability) is used in many parts of the world. Even relatively obscure grains, like triticale, spelt, and emmer have found their way into horses' diets.

Oats (*Avena sativa*) are the traditional favorite, reported to make up more than 30% of all commercially prepared horse feeds. The same quality that makes them such a popular feed for horses is responsible for their being less favored for other livestock: they have a low energy density compared to most other grains. That's a result of the fibrous hull, which makes up a significant portion of the oat seed and makes oats a "safer" feed for horses (less likely to cause cecal acidosis, because of a lower starch content) than hull-less grains such as corn and wheat.

Horses seem to prefer oats.

Horses also seem to prefer oats over most other grains, making them a close second in the palatability sweepstakes to molasses-laced sweet feeds. But oats tend to vary more in quality and price than most other grain crops, and the yield per acre is relatively low. Their popularity with owners and trainers, in many cases, seems to have more to do with habit and a lack of familiarity with other cereal grains than anything else.

Because oats have a relatively soft kernel, most adult horses have no difficulty chewing and digesting them. Oats can be "clipped" (a process in which the pointed top and tail of the grain are clipped off), "crimped" (lightly crushed so as to crack, but not completely remove, the hull), or rolled (to make oatmeal), but these processing techniques are rarely needed to make oats a good horse feed, except in the case of very young or very old equines, or those with tooth problems.

Oats have the advantage of being less vulnerable to molds and mycotoxins than most other grains. But because of their relatively small growing area (they grow best in cool weather, limiting their cultivation to the northern States and southern Canada) and low yields, oats are becoming less and less popular as a major crop — which means that oats are more expensive than other grains, and likely to become more so.

It pays to shop for good quality, "heavy" oats (sometimes called "racehorse oats") because they contain less foreign material and weigh more per unit of volume. The individual grains should look plump, light blonde in color, and fairly uniform in size. Slimmer, lightweight oats may provide the same nutrition but less value for your dollar.

Dehulled oats, sometimes called groats, are an alternative feed sometimes available for horses. They provide more digestible energy per pound but lack the safety margin that the oat hull provides. That, coupled with the high cost of processing the grains this way, makes groats a far less popular feed for horses than they were in the past.

Corn (*Zea mays*), or maize, as it's known in many parts of the world, is probably the second most familiar grain for horses, and overall as a livestock feed, it is the leading crop in the United States. It constitutes more than 80% of the grain fed to animals in North America, and its production continues to rise. Most horses find it only slightly less palatable than oats and tastier than many other cereal grains. Plus, it is a good-quality and nutritious grain for horses.

Because corn is a hull-less grain, however, it is very high in starches. Fiber makes up only 2.2% of its total composition, and its digestible energy (DE) value is more than twice that of oats. This means that it does not have the "safety margin" that oats enjoy, and it must be fed with caution and in relatively small quantities. Many nutritionists recommend against corn's being fed as the sole grain for this reason, suggesting that it is best mixed with other grains to balance its high starch concentration.

Corn is a good quality, nutritious grain.

Corn's reputation for being a feed that makes horses "hot" and hard to handle is largely a myth; it stems from owners who have carelessly substituted corn for an equal quantity of oats in their horse's diets — unwittingly supplying more than twice the energy! Feeding by weight, rather than by volume, is crucial when switching grains.

The hardness of the individual kernels means that in order to be digested well by the horse, corn usually needs to be processed, by cracking (breaking each kernel into pieces), or flaking (flattening kernels with a roller). That processing increases the utilization of the grain but also exposes it to the possible growth of molds and mycotoxins that can cause aflatoxicosis and moldy corn disease (both potentially fatal) if ingested. Of all the cereal grains fed to horses, corn is the most likely to be contaminated by molds, particularly if poorly stored (in very damp, humid, or hot conditions). Because of this threat, any corn even remotely questionable should never be fed.

But contrary to popular belief, corn is not a "heating" feed in the traditional sense. In fact, because the greatest amount of internal heat in the horse's body is generated through the microbial fermentation of fiber, not starches, increasing the amount of hay in your horse's diet in winter will generate more body heat than will increasing the amount of corn he eats. However, because corn pro-

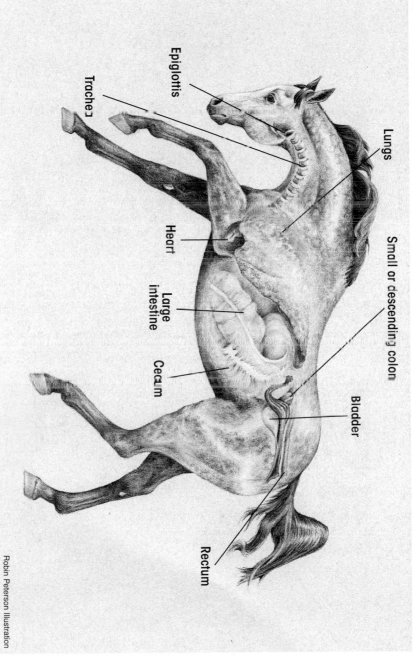

Epiglottis

Trachea

Lungs

Heart

Small or descending colon

Large intestine

Cecum

Bladder

Rectum

Viscera of the Horse

Robin Peterson Illustration

The horse in the photo above is in poor condition as evidenced
by coat condition and prominence of ribs and hips;
the horse below is lean but racing fit.

The horse in the photo above is in excellent condition and carrying an appropriate amount of weight for his size; the horse below is overweight — notice the thickness of the neck and fat deposits on the hindquarters.

By late fall, the nutrient value of this pasture has dropped considerably; below, hay cut past mid-bloom is stemmy and contains a number of sud-heads, an indication that the nutritive value of the hay is past its best.

In winter, horses that live outside need forage, and hay provides that requirement; below, weanlings get valuable nutrients from pasture grass and hay.

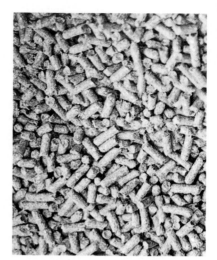

Clockwise from top left: beet pulp, "complete feed,"
barley, and extruded feed.

A well-organized feed room (above);
below, sweet feed, a staple in many barns.

Horses not only love apples and treats such as carrots, but they get important nutrients from these sources.

vides lots of energy per pound, and energy needs increase during cold weather, corn is a good winter feed for horses.

Very popular in the United Kingdom and Europe as a horse feed, barley (*Hordeum vulgare*) doesn't enjoy the same favor on this side of the Atlantic. However, it has a long and honored history on the equine bill of fare, even being reputed to have been the staple diet for the early Arabian herds that laid the foundation for so many modern horse breeds. Today, it's the most widely cultivated cereal grain in the world, needing a shorter growing season than corn and tolerating limited rainfall well. Over half of the world's harvest of barley comes from Europe and the former Soviet Union. In the United States, about half of the total barley crop (only about one-twentieth of the corn harvest) is fed to livestock, with another 25% going toward alcohol production.

Barley grains resemble smallish oats, but are harder. Because of this, they usually are rolled or crimped when fed to horses. (In the UK, it's common to cook the barley grains, making the starches more digestible and the meal far more palatable.) Processed barley can be dusty, and if finely ground, the end product, which is heavy and low in bulk, might tend to pack in the stomach and present a colic risk. For this reason, when barley is fed as the principal grain, it's often mixed with a fibrous product such as chopped hay or straw (chaff), or beet pulp, to keep the digestive system moving everything along. It's also used as a major component in commercial pelleted feeds.

Like oats, most types of barley contain hulls, providing the grain with a higher fiber content than corn, but lower than oats. In fact, barley could be described as an "in-between" grain in many ways — supplying more digestible energy and total digestible nutrients (TDN) than the same quantity of oats, but not as much as corn — and between oats and corn in terms of fiber content and "safety," as well as heat produced in its digestion. But it's slightly higher in protein than either oats or corn (making it a good choice for breeding stock and young horses), has a very high phosphorus content (so high, in fact, that it is undesirable as a single grain even when fed with high-calcium alfalfa to balance it out), and less of its starch tends to be processed in the small intestine, increasing the risk of cecal acidosis. In addition, barley is less palatable than oats and corn and is most commonly used in a grain mix with oats, corn, and frequently molasses.

Grain sorghum, or milo (*S. vulgare*), represents about 6% to 8% of the grain fed to livestock in the United States, and it can make a good feed for horses, though its feed value varies depending on its tannin content. Tannins provide a degree of resistance to mold, but decrease milo's protein digestibility and palatability, as well as giving it an astringent taste. Brown milo, which has the highest concentration of tannins, is not a suitable feed for horses because of this. (Unfortunately, yellow milo, the preferred variety, is often difficult to differentiate visually from brown.)

Milo has a small, hard kernel, and for efficient use by horses, it must be steam-flaked. Whole grains, or even those that have been dry rolled, are too difficult for horses to chew and digest. Like corn, milo is high in energy density and low in fiber, so it must be fed with caution.

In addition to the grains described above, wheat, rye, and even hulled rice all can make suitable additions to the horse's diet, but they seldom are fed in North America, either because their palatability is low or because their cost and/or availability are prohibitive. However, they occasionally make an appearance on the feed label of a commercially mixed ration.

Processing Grains

The practice of processing grains sometimes can markedly improve their digestibility, but it is not without its disadvantages. Chief among these is the fact that when you break the hard coat that is the seed's natural protection, you make it vulnerable to invasion from microorganisms as well as insects. You also open the endosperm to more rapid nutrient breakdown on exposure to the elements. At the very least, breaking open the kernel exposes the grain to oxidation, causing a stale flavor that quickly decreases its palatability. (Some feed companies apply antioxidants and mold inhibitors to their processed grains to combat this.) Grains that have been crimped, rolled, steamed, or otherwise processed must be stored for much shorter periods than whole grains and must be watched closely for signs of mold.

In the case of oats, no increase in feeding value has been noted for processed (crimped, rolled, or steam flaked) oats vs. whole grains — and most nutritionists recommend that oats only be processed for those horses with dental problems. But in the case of harder grains, such as barley and corn, processing can provide significant advantages in terms of the amount of starch digested in the small intestine (as opposed to the cecum), and reduce the risk of diarrhea, colic, and founder. For small hard grains, such as milo, rye, and wheat, processing is essential for horses to extract any nutrient value.

Methods of processing can include cracking and rolling of the dry grains to varying degrees. The grains should not be finely ground, as this decreases palatability and increases the dustiness of the ration; in addition, some researchers suspect it might contribute to gastric ulcers as it does in pigs. In any case, the use of finely ground grain is no better (and possibly worse) than more coarsely ground kernels. Larger pieces of the individual kernels also make it easier for you to assess the quality of the grain.

Heat processing, which can include steam-flaking, micronizing, pelleting, and extruding almost invariably makes grain more expensive, but it also offers some pluses. Studies have shown that protein use from both oats and milo is 2% to 3% higher when these grains are micronized (cooked with dry-heat microwaves), and starch digestion of corn in the small intestine was improved by almost three times when the grain was extruded. In addition, most horses show a marked preference for processed grains over unprocessed ones, in the case of every grain except oats.

Which to Buy?

Although all of the grains discussed here can have a valuable place in your horse's diet, no single grain will provide all the nutrients a working horse needs, even when fed in combination with premium-quality hay. Of all the grains commonly fed to horses, oats are generally considered the closest to the "perfect" feed, but even oats fail to supply sufficient quantities of many vitamins and minerals, and their relative energy density is low (which as we know, makes them safer but more expensive to feed, pound per pound).

This is the point where commercially balanced rations offer a tremendous advantage. Formulated with a mix of grains, and generally supplemented with a mixture of vitamins and minerals appropriate to the type of horse it is designed for (i.e. performance horses, breeding stock, or growing youngsters), a commercial ration provides what no single grain can: balanced nutrition. Commercially prepared feeds take a lot of the guesswork out of calculating whether your horse is receiving all the vitamins and minerals he needs. Feed companies employ Ph.D. nutritionists to formulate such feeds, and the end result is a ration that needs no added powders or potions to provide complete nutrition.

You can, of course, also do your own calculations and create your own balanced feed from a mixture of grains, but the math can sometimes be daunting and the results dependent on how complete your understanding of nutrition is. However, it's comforting to know that from crop to crop, the nutrient values listed in charts like the one on page 125 are far more reliable for grain than for hay (the content of which can fluctuate wildly depending on the soil, growing conditions, and season). If you are interested in formulating your own ration, consult your feed company's equine specialist or your state extension specialist (whom you can locate by contacting the nearest university with an agricultural college). He or she can help provide you with reliable information on how to tailor a grain ration to your horse's needs.

The most popular format for a mixed feed is what the feed industry calls a "textured ration," and what most of us know as "sweet feed." Sweet feed is simply a mixture of grains, with a touch of sweet flavoring, usually molasses, added to improve palatability, reduce dustiness, and bind the mixture. Within that description, there's room for an infinite number of variations, depending on the ingredients used. Some sweet feeds are basic in the extreme while others feature lots of nutritional bells and whistles — a pumped-up vitamin and mineral supplement, perhaps some added fats and oils, and/or extra fiber, in the form of dehydrated alfalfa or shredded beet pulp. Most sweet feeds also include a preservative to prevent spoilage. The chemical-phobic can take heart, however: Often, the

feed industry uses a natural anti-oxidant, such as vitamin E, to do the job.

When selecting a sweet feed, use all of your senses. Look for healthy, plump individual grains in the mix, a pleasantly sweet smell, and very little in the way of dust or fines. Most sweet feeds have a shelf life of about six months (or three months if fat-supplemented), but any sign of moldiness or insect contamination means the feed should be discarded. Generally, beware of feeds that

Sweet feed is the most popular format for a mixed feed.

have very heavy molasses — not only is such a mix very difficult to work with, sticking to everything in summer and freezing solid in the winter, but it is more prone to spoilage. In addition, molasses can very well disguise inferior ingredients and a high dust content. It is often a sign of a multitude of sins being committed at the feed mill! You are better to pay a little more for a feed with high-quality ingredients that don't need camouflage.

Pelleted Feeds

Almost as familiar a sight in the average feed room as sweet feed, is a bag of small, cylindrical shapes called pellets. Pelleting, a versatile technology, is used for everything from rabbit feed to parrot and monkey chow, and it's been a popular option for horse rations for many years now.

Granted, pelleted feeds don't usually exude the tempting aroma of most molasses-laced sweet feeds, but they more than make up for that in terms of convenience and digestibility. Feed mills have learned to apply pelleting techniques to practically every type of feed a horse can consume, from hay to grains to combinations of the two (often called "complete" feeds). Almost no commercial feed ration is left untouched by the pelleting process — sift through a prepared sweet feed with your fingers, and you'll likely discover a smattering of pellets mixed in with the oats and corn and other grains. That pellet generally contains a vitamin/mineral supplement for the ration, bound up with a fiber source such as dehydrated alfalfa.

Pellets are made by first grinding the grain into particles of a uniform size — not too fine and not too coarse. The particles then are combined with a "binder," for horse feed. Most companies use natural binders as much as possible — wheat, in particular, is an excellent binder, which helps make a hard, durable pellet, and barley also does a creditable job. So does molasses, a naturally sticky product that does double duty as a flavoring agent.

In the case of a recipe that has little in the way of ingredients that are natural binders, manufacturers may add an artificial binder, usually a product called "lignasol," which is a fine yellow powder. Widely used in other livestock feeds because it is less expensive than natural binders, and because it is easy to work with, lignasol has a limited use in horse feeds because there is a consumer perception that "natural" is better — and horse feed recipes are far more driven by consumer opinion than are, for instance, cattle feeds.

In a mixing chamber, the ground particles are churned together and compacted, and the binder is mixed through (except in the case of a "wet" binder like molasses, which is generally added during "conditioning," the next step in the process). Then the particles move on to a "pellet mill conditioner," where forced steam heats them to a temperature of 180 to 190 degrees Fahrenheit, for about 20 seconds. (Longer exposure to the steam has been found to make a more durable pellet, so some newer mills are now equipped with "double pass" steaming chambers, a process that steams the ingredients twice.) Steaming gelatinizes the starches in the grain, which makes it stick together, and helps it slip through the die (metal plate with holes that create the pellet shape) better. The objective is not to cook the grain, which would destroy vitamins and minerals, but to break the bonds in the complex starches; some researchers feel this increases the overall digestibility of the grain as well. (Increased digestibility of gelatinized starches has been demonstrated in dogs, cats, pigs, and poultry, but the jury is still out with regard to ruminants and horses.)

The next step is pushing the feed (at relatively low pressure) through the die. The size of the holes determines the size of the resulting pellet, and many manufacturers attempt to mark their products with a pellet of distinct dimensions, anywhere from about the thickness of a pencil to about the thickness of your thumb. Pelleted products designed for foals are sometimes finer than those made for adult horses.

The pellets then drop into a pellet mill cooler, where excess moisture is drawn out until the product contains less than 15.5% moisture overall. This step is essential to prevent mold growth. Once this step is accomplished, pelleted feeds have little chance of going moldy unless they are stored in damp conditions. Before being bagged, the pellets undergo one final step in their journey through the mill: They travel through a pellet shaker, a device like a giant sifter that removes the small chips and fines from the intact pellets and recycles them into the next batch.

A number of factors determine how hard and durable, or how

soft and crumbly, a pellet is, including the amount of exposure to steam, the retention time in the die, moisture levels in the feed, the ambient temperature and humidity, and the type and amount of the binder. Feed mills can now actually measure the relative durability of a pellet. If the durability is unacceptable, the feed is recycled and reprocessed. Not only does a soft pellet tend to be dusty, but it's generally considered less toothsome to horses, which show a marked preference for harder, crunchier pellets as a rule.

Advantages of Pelleted Feeds

• Pelleted feeds are significantly less dusty than unprocessed grains. This can be an important factor if you are feeding a horse with respiratory problems. Because pellets are not coated with molasses, as are most commercial sweet feeds, they are also easier to handle in the winter.

• Horses can't sort ingredients in a pelleted feed. If you have a picky eater that likes to sort all the oats out of his sweet feed and leave the rest, he is likely not getting the nutrition the ration is designed to deliver. With a pellet, he has no choice but to eat the whole thing. The unpleasant taste or texture of some ingredients, such as fats and oils, can also be "disguised" in a pelleted ration and ingested more readily than they would if top-dressed.

• Because pellets are relatively low in moisture, feeding them tends to result in reduced manure output — especially in the case of hay pellets. The advantages of this need hardly be explained to anyone who has ever wielded a muck fork! Some researchers feel, however, that this may increase the risk of impaction in some horses; studies are currently examining the question.

• Because pellets are made up of feed ground into particles, they are, in a manner of speaking "pre-chewed." This makes them a much more digestible choice than whole grains or hay for very young or old horses, or for any horse with a mouth or tooth problem. Pellets can also be soaked into a mush to be fed to elderly horses that have little or no grinding surfaces left on their teeth. (Pellets have not been shown to increase overall digestibility of a ration when fed to adult horses with no chewing difficulties, however.)

Disadvantages of Pelleted Feeds

• Some researchers feel that because horses tend to eat pellets more quickly than they do unprocessed feeds, this format also might increase the risk of digestive upset, as the finer particles can have a tendency to pack in the gut. However, studies have demonstrated no difference in the rate of intestinal fermentation between sweet feeds and pelleted feeds — an argument against an increased risk of colic. These results are still open to interpretation.

• Because they are compacted and bulky, pellets can carry a slightly increased risk of choke, especially in horses that bolt their feed. Strategies to help address this problem include placing a few large, smooth stones in the feed tub; feeding little amounts and often; mixing in some chaff, chopped hay, or soaked beet pulp; and placing some bars across the feed tub, similar to a foal feeder. Or try this: Choose smallish pellets and spread them out thinly in a large, shallow feed tub to make your horse slow down and work for his meal.

• Assessing the quality of a pelleted product can be difficult because the ingredients are compacted and ground. The manufacturer's nutritional analysis (printed on the bag or on a feed tag attached to the product) should provide you with some assurance, but the only way to be sure of the quality of a pelleted ration is to examine it visually for a firm (not crumbly) texture, a pleasant smell, no visible signs of mold, weeds, or foreign material, and few fines (small dusty particles)… and to send a sample of the product for a nutritional analysis by a commercial or university laboratory. Buying from a reputable manufacturer offering a product guarantee can go a long way toward your peace of mind.

• The cost of processing a grain pellet will almost always push the price of such a ration up past what unprocessed feeds would cost.

Extruded Feeds

A more recent addition to the world of horse feeds is the extruded feed. Extruded products look like dog kibble (they're made by the same process). They're largish, spherical, lightweight pieces of uniform color, hard and somewhat crunchy in texture. In the United Kingdom, they are sometimes called "pony nuts." Extruded products are made by the same basic process that produces pellets, with one important difference: The mix is forced through the die openings under high pressure. When the feed emerges from the die, the sudden release of this pressure causes the particles to expand, almost like popping corn. As a result, extruded products are about half as dense as pelleted products or sweet feeds made with the same ingredients.

Because extruded feeds are made up of fairly large individual particles, they take longer for a horse to chew. This can be a significant advantage for horses that tend to bolt their feed or that colic easily. However, many horses find the shape and texture strange at first. They might require some time to become accustomed to it. And because the "kernels" of extruded feeds are less dense, you get less feed value per bag — often at the same price. Still, extruded products are very spoilage-resistant, and many horses seem to maintain their weight well on them, making them a popular choice.

Whatever the format, when you buy grain, trust your senses. If it doesn't look or smell palatable to you, you probably don't want to feed it to your horses. Buy only the best-quality grain you can afford, buy it in small quantities whenever possible to ensure freshness, and store it properly.

Comparative Values for Grains Commonly Fed to Horses

Grain	Relative Feeding Value by volume (%)	Decrease in density if ground (%)	Crude Protein (%)	Crude Fiber (%)	Comments
Oats (regular)	45	28	11-12	11	Most palatable and safest grain — often most expensive and variable in quality.
Oats (heavy)	50	20	12.5	11	Also called "racehorse" or "jockey" oats.
Groats (hull-less oats)	95		18	2.4	
Corn (maize)	100	14	8-10	2.2	Grain most prone to mold and most commonly overfed.
Barley	85	25	12	5	Between oats and corn in safety, but less palatable.
Sorghum (milo)	95		11.5	2.6	Should be processed. Brown variety is high-tannin, less digestible and less palatable.
Wheat	110	14	11-14	1.5-3	Less palatable than corn or oats. Should be processed.
Rye	100	14	12	2.2	Feed processed, with 1/3 maximum in grain mix. Ensure no ergot (a poisonous fungus).
Wheat bran			16-17	10-12	Not a laxative. When fed, ensure there is as much Ca as P in the total diet.
Rice bran			14	13	Fed as a fat supplement (fat content 15% dry matter). Ca:P imbalance similar to wheat bran.

From *Feeding and Care of the Horse* (1996), 2nd. ed., by Lon D. Lewis DVM, Ph.D., Dipl. ACVN. (Page 71, Table 4-5)

Ration Balancing

Here's where we put it all together. It's time to take all of that information from our preceding chapters and formulate some balanced diets for our horses. At this point most people freeze in fear!

Relax. It's true that there are all sorts of complicated calculations you can do to determine optimum levels of every essential nutrient, but it's also true that 90% of the time, you don't need to perform any convoluted math to ensure your equines' good health. Your horse will tell you if he's receiving good nutrition — by his shiny coat, good appetite, pleasant outlook, and appropriate energy level. If you are feeding average-to-excellent quality forage and grain, you can be reasonably assured that your horse's diet will meet his daily nutrient requirements. This is nearly always the case when you feed a commercial ration without supplements; only during growth (especially in the first year), lactation, and the last three months of pregnancy are horses likely to need extra nutritional support. Supplementing also might be necessary if the forage you're feeding is of poor quality (assuming, of course, that you're unable to replace it with something better).

It's worth noting, however, that contrary to popular belief, horses do not have "nutritional wisdom" when it comes to their diets. Some marketing pros would have you believe that horses instinctively choose the plants and nutrients they need for good health. Alas, that's not the case — if it were true, we would never have a problem with horses gorging them-selves with grain until they colic. With the exception of salt and water, horses do not develop cravings for the nutrients they require; they simply function according to appetite and taste preference, just as we do.

A horse's daily menu needs to include about 40 different nutrients in all: the proper amounts of energy and protein; 15 different minerals, plus chlorine;

AT A GLANCE

◆ A horse's daily menu should include approximately 40 different nutrients.

◆ The total weight of feed per day should be between 1.5% and 3.0% of a horse's body weight.

◆ A horse's nutritional needs depend on the type of work he does.

◆ Several methods, besides a scale, can determine a horse's body weight.

14 different vitamins, plus beta-carotene; fat; water; and at least four amino acids (lysine, methionine, tryptophane, and threonine). Fortunately, as we know, any common equine diet provides most of these in adequate amounts. The only ones that might be inadequate or excessive are protein, digestible energy (DE), calcium, phosphorus, and selenium. For growing horses, add zinc and copper to that list; for adult horses, the levels of these two minerals are generally adequate in any diet. Levels of vitamins A and E also can be a concern for growing horses and those in high-performance situations in the winter months when they have no access to growing forage. So it's only these nutrients that need to be taken into consideration when formulating a ration.

Before you get out your calculator, you need to know a few basic things:

1) What stage of life is your horse in? Are you feeding a growing foal, a lactating broodmare, an adult pleasure horse, or a hundred-mile endurance champion? Your horse's status will have an important bearing on the nutrients required.

2) Is your horse idle or doing work of light, medium, or serious intensity? Is his workload due to be increased, decreased, or remain constant?

3) Is your horse in the condition you'd like him to be? Is he too fat or too thin? (See the chart at the end of this chapter to "condition

score" your horse. The ideal is a "5.")

4) What feeds are available to you? Which are reasonably priced? There is no use formulating a ration based on ingredients you can't get or that are outrageously expensive.

Next, you need to know your horse's body weight. The most accurate way to determine his weight is to stand him on a scale specifically designed for horses, but you'll likely only have access to this piece of equipment if you are lucky enough to live near a university veterinary school. A rough approximation of your horse's weight can be obtained by using the "heart girth" measuring tapes sold at many feed stores for a couple of dollars, though these are sometimes "off" by more than a hundred pounds (and incidentally, are useless for pregnant mares, whose heart girth alone will not tell the story). A more accurate result can be obtained by using the following relatively simple formula:

$$\text{Body weight in lbs.} = \frac{[\,(\text{heart girth in inches})^2 \times \text{length in inches}\,]}{330}$$

where the length of your horse is measured from the front point of his shoulder blade to the point of his rump.

If you prefer to do metric calculations, use:

$$\text{Body weight in kg} = \frac{[\,(\text{heart-girth in cm})^2 \times \text{length in cm}]}{11{,}880}$$

For light-horse foals one to six weeks of age, use:

$$\text{Body weight in lbs.} = \frac{[\text{heart girth in inches} - 25.1]}{0.07}$$

or

$$\text{Bodyweight in kg} = \frac{[\text{heart girth in cm} - 63.7]}{0.38.}$$

It's worth doing these calculations because once you have your horse's weight you can use a simple rule of thumb to determine how much feed your horse should be getting each day. The total weight of feed per day should be between 1.5% and 3.0% of your horse's body weight.

For example, a 950-pound Morgan gelding would need between 14.25 pounds and 28.5 pounds of total feed (forage plus grain). That's a good bit of leeway, of course, and it allows some adjustability. For example, if our Morgan was overweight and only in light work, you would lean toward the lower end of the scale, at 14.25 pounds a day. If, on the other hand, he was in top physical condition and was competing in a high-intensity sport such as endurance racing or upper-level combined driving, he might require closer to 28 pounds of feed a day to provide him with the energy he needs.

The 1.5% to 3.0% rule works for almost all types of horses, except for nursing foals (who will only eat between 0.5% to 0.75% of their bodyweight in solid food while they are nursing) and weanlings, which might consume up to 3.5% of their bodyweight per day. The chart at the end of this chapter shows how the intake will vary, depending on the horse's activity and energy requirements. Intense work, lactation (nursing), and growth all need to be fueled by larger amounts of nutrients. To some extent, the intake also will be affected by temperament (laid-back, easy keepers will be at the lower end of the scale while nervous or high-strung horses that are hard keepers will need more) and climate (because it takes more energy to maintain internal body temperature in below-freezing weather).

To use the rule effectively, you will have to weigh your horse's feed. Most horsemen, of course, don't operate this systematically — we're used to just estimating by the "coffee can" method of measuring (this horse gets half a scoop; this one a whole scoop; that pony a handful). Rest assured that weighing the ration need not be a daily routine — once you've done it a few times, you should be able to estimate the amount fairly effectively. But it's important to weigh both the hay and the grain your horse receives at least a few times; otherwise, your guesstimates might not be very accurate.

Hay bales can vary in weight from less than 40 pounds to more than 100 pounds. They also vary in terms of the number of flakes they contain. The simplest way to determine their weight is to bring your bathroom scale out to the barn. Stand on it empty-handed to find your own weight; then repeat the process while hoisting a bale of hay. Subtract your weight from the weight of you holding the bale to get the hay's weight. Then crack open a couple of bales and weigh yourself holding some representative flakes. Find an average of the weights, and you'll have a much better idea how much hay you're really feeding your horse when you toss him three flakes in the evening.

Weighing grain is done most easily with an ordinary kitchen scale. (Be sure to subtract the weight of the empty container you use to scoop your grain.) Remember that some grains are far more energy dense than others, so any time you substitute one type of grain for another, you should repeat the weighing process to make sure that you're delivering an equivalent weight, not an equivalent volume. A one-quart scoop of corn will have considerably more energy than a one-quart scoop of oats — so if you feed that quart to a horse used to eating oats, you could have one excitable horse on your hands! (Keep in mind that it takes many days for a horse to adjust to changes in the energy content of his diet — so if you change feeds, do so gradually.)

We know from our chapter on fiber that under almost all circumstances, a horse's diet should consist of at least 50% forage. (The only exceptions are weanlings and yearlings, for which grain might make up 70% and 60%, respectively, of their total diet as a maximum; and 2-year-olds in intense race training, which might receive up to 65% grain if necessary.) So of the 1.5% to 3% total feed an adult horse consumes daily, he should receive a minimum of 0.75% pasture, hay, or other fiber sources. He could, of course, receive up to 3% pasture or hay, if he is an easy keeper and/or idle or in light work. Going back to our 950-pound Morgan gelding, if we assume he, like most other Morgans, is easy to keep weight on, and if we know he is used for pleasure riding only, he could survive quite nicely on 14.25 pounds of forage per day. If, on the other hand, he is very fit and is competing at the highest levels of combined driving, he might need a daily diet consisting of 14.25 pounds of hay and another 14.25 pounds of grain to fuel his performance (for a total of 28.5 pounds of feed, or 3% of his bodyweight). When you do these figures, remember there's some room for adjustment — and that you also can factor in a 10% to 15% wastage factor for hay.

If you have good-quality pasture and/or hay and are feeding a well-formulated commercial grain mix, you might never need to do more ration balancing than the above. To make sure your horse is getting enough protein, calcium, and phosphorus, use the chart at the end of the chapter — and compare the requirements to the total amount in the diet you're providing. For example, if you are feeding your breeding stallion a legume hay with 15% crude protein (a figure you'll know from having run a hay analysis), and it makes up 50% of his ration, choose a low-protein grain (under 10%) to balance that high-protein hay. If, on the other hand, you are feeding a grass hay with only 8% crude protein, you can afford to offer a higher-protein grain ration. Under most circumstances, of course, it's very difficult to create a protein deficiency in an adult horse; but with a young, growing horse, or a mare that is nursing or in the last stage of pregnancy, protein, calcium, and phosphorus values are more crucial. Selecting a grain mix designed for the stage of life your horse is in is the easiest approach here — it can save you a lot of trouble (not to mention your calculator batteries).

Special Cases

High performance: The more work a horse does, the higher his energy requirement. While it's possible to calculate the exact digestible energy your horse's diet delivers, for the average horse owner, listening to your horse is enough. If, as his workload is intensified, he is becoming fatigued earlier than you'd like or if he's losing weight, it's time to supply more energy to the diet. That means increasing the amount of carbohydrates and fats he receives (which might necessitate reducing the amount of hay or forage he eats if you're nearing the 3% limit). If you have a high-performance horse

already close to receiving the maximum amount of grain he should eat on a daily basis, however, consider adding some supplemental fat, in the form of vegetable oil, to his diet. As we noted in the chapter on feeding fat, fat takes some time to "kick in," but it is an excellent energy source, supplying almost two and a half times the energy of carbohydrates. It can provide an energy boost without increasing the overall volume of feed by more than an ounce or two.

High performance = high energy requirements.

Pregnancy and lactation: During the first trimester of pregnancy, a mare's nutritional needs are not much different than they would normally be. From about the fifth month on, however, the fetus makes significant demands on her body. By the final trimester (from about day 240 of the pregnancy on), most researchers recommend a 2% rise in the level of crude protein a mare receives (from 8% to 10%), as well as an 85% increase in the amount of calcium, and a 100% increase in the amount of phosphorus. Copper, zinc, manganese, and iron are important for good bone and muscle growth and maturation in the foal and are best supplied at this time as they are only present in low concentrations in mare's milk. In the 11th month, a further increase in protein level, to 11%, is recommended. Energy requirements in the mare also increase by about 20% in the last trimester. Typically, rations need to be changed from an early-pregnancy diet of about 80% to 90% forage to a 70% forage/30% concentrates diet as foaling approaches.

Also, keep in mind that mares in late gestation usually are being fed hay that has been in storage longer than three months. This means some deterioration of the fat-soluble vitamins A, D, and E. A commercially prepared vitamin supplement for broodmares can be an excellent addition to the diet at this time. (Problems with retained placentas after the foal is born also are linked to inadequate selenium, calcium, and vitamin E in the diet — another good reason to supplement before foaling.)

Lactation, to many people's surprise, is actually more stressful to the mare than pregnancy. During the first three months of nursing her foal, she will need significant nutritional support, including a diet that has 13% crude protein, high digestible energy (this is also a good time for a high-fat diet), and calcium

Nursing mares need nutritional support.

and phosphorus levels of at least 0.5% and 0.35%. She also will need more total calories and should be fed between 2.5% and 3.0% of her bodyweight in total feed per day. After the third month, as her foal eats more solid food and nurses less often, her milk production gradually decreases, as do her nutrient and energy requirements. By the time the foal is weaned, she should be back to "pre-pregnancy" status in terms of her diet, regardless of whether she is open or was re-bred. If she is pregnant, the cycle of extra nutritional support will recur when she reaches the ninth-month stage.

Nursing foals: Because they are growing so rapidly, young foals have the highest nutrient and energy requirements of any other age of horse. Continuing good nutritional support of the mare will ensure that the foal receives good nutrition in his milk, and most researchers recommend the use of a creep feed for foals as well. Such a feed is usually manufactured with a protein level of 16% to 18% and includes milk protein, which has an optimal amino acid profile including high levels of lysine. Look, as well, for a calcium level close to, or even exceeding 0.9% and a phosphorus level of 0.6% or better (but never exceeding the calcium level). Copper levels of upward of 50 ppm are also a good idea, particularly if you live in an area with copper-deficient soils; and zinc levels, which affect copper absorption, should also be high, in the 60 ppm range.

At three to four weeks old, foals should be introduced to creep feed, and at first they likely will consume only about 300 g (a little over half a pound). By three or four months of age, though, they'll be eating more than a kilogram (2.2 pounds) a day, and be at three to four kilograms (6.6 to 8.8 pounds) by the time they're weaned. Yeast culture, an inexpensive feed supplement that improves phosphorus utilization and the overall digestibility of grains, and also provides extra B vitamins, is a good idea for weanlings, as is a good-quality legume forage such as alfalfa hay. (See chapter 12 for further notes on feeding foals to prevent developmental orthopedic disease.)

Breeding stallions: Many researchers feel that a breeding stallion benefits from some supplemental protein (to 10%) and slightly elevated calcium and phosphorus levels. Breeding seems to be harder on some stallions than on others, with some becoming quite ribby over the course of the breeding season; others positively thrive on the routine and need their grain cut back a little. Once the breeding season is over, a stallion should be maintained like any other adult horse, according to his work level.

The "hot" horse: Many owners complain that their horses are too hot, or high-strung, to work with easily, and diet often gets the blame. The type of horse that tends to be hot also tends to be difficult to keep weight on (often a Thoroughbred or Thoroughbred-cross). This is something of a Catch-22 — if you reduce the feed, the horse is more manageable but loses weight; increase the feed, and the horse maintains his weight but is wired for sound! Take heart; there are solutions.

Being hot is often, at least, partly a function of temperament, but feeding more energy than the horse can expend constructively doesn't help. To find a healthier compromise, provide the hot horse with as much exercise as possible (that includes both work and turn-out time), and adjust his diet so that he receives enough total food to keep his ribs covered, while delivering a more appropriate energy level. Reducing the amount of grain while adding beet pulp to the grain ration is one popular solution — in this way, you're supplementing the amount of low-energy, filling fiber your horse receives, but as it's mixed in with his grain, he hardly misses what he's not getting. Supplemental fat can also be useful here to help keep weight on because any not used as an energy source is easily stored as fat (just as it does — far too easily — in our own bodies). The hot horse also benefits from generous quantities of forage. And if the horse still has too much energy for the work he does ... well, perhaps he's in the wrong line of work. He may be a square peg in a round hole as a Western pleasure horse, for example, but would find a happy home as an eventer or polo pony.

The overweight horse: The answer is as simple, and difficult, as it is for humans. Eat less and more exercise! Certain types of horses seem to be "air ferns" — they can survive, and become quite plump, on a diet that seems to provide far too little for the average horse. Some pony breeds, in particular, have to be managed very carefully because they are at greater risk of laminitis if they consume large amounts of grain, or even graze on sweet spring grass. As cruel as it might sound, keeping such a horse or pony on a "dry lot" rather than a pasture with good grazing can be healthier — at least until the rich new growth has stopped in the heat of the summer. Careful monitoring of the amount of forage consumed should be coupled with lots of exercise. And unless the horse is in intense work, he can probably get by with no grain at all. To ensure he is receiving a correct complement of vitamins and minerals, look for a supplement designed to balance a high-forage diet; many feed companies have such supplements available.

The older horse: Advances in medical treatment as well as nutrition mean we have more geriatric horses with us than ever before. This is not necessarily a bad thing; many horses in their 20s and 30s continue to be productive individuals whose wisdom and patience make them a joy to have around. But as a horse ages, his nutritional needs change, and we cannot merely assume that what worked in the past will work in the future. Older horses tend to have dental problems; often, the grinding surfaces have worn down so much that they lose much of their ability to chew fibrous matter like hay. This can be a primary cause of an older horse's inability to maintain good condition. In addition, the internal organs become less efficient at digesting nutrients — particularly, protein, phosphorus, and fiber. Because of this, it's worth seeking out a feed that offers slightly higher levels of these nutrients and is relatively soft and easy to chew; a number of feed companies now offer formulas specifically designed for geriatrics, though any pelleted ration will likely be a better choice than unprocessed whole grains.

Choosing a soft, leafy hay with a higher concentration of legumes is also a good idea as your older horse may have trouble chewing and digesting a stemmy, fibrous grass hay. And if your horse has trouble maintaining his weight, particularly in the winter months, the addition of some vegetable oil to the diet (up to two cups a day, depending on his size) can provide him with more energy and calories.

Extremely aged horses, with no teeth to speak of, can sometimes be maintained quite comfortably by soaking forage and grain to make a "mush." Hay cubes, soaked in warm water for an hour or so before feeding, become quite manageable, and beet pulp can help provide more fiber; pelleted grains also can be soaked to make them much easier to chew.

Regular veterinary maintenance is also a good idea for an older horse. He may need his teeth floated on a quarterly instead of twice-yearly basis, and it's useful to run a blood profile periodically as well, to pick up "red flags" such as impaired liver or kidney function. (Horses with renal or liver failure cannot tolerate high levels of protein and may need other dietary adjustments as well.)

Feeding in cold weather: When the thermometer plunges, horses have to work harder to maintain their internal body temperatures. To keep them from losing weight, you'll need to provide more calories about 15 to 20% more feed per day for every 10 degree (Fahrenheit) drop in the temperature below 30 degrees F. Hay, not grain, is the better choice for helping your horse generate body heat because fibrous feeds are slowly digested in the cecum by bacterial fermentation, a process that generates lots of warmth. Grain is digested quickly, so it creates less heat. To help your horse stay warm, first increase the amount of hay he receives. (If you feed your hay outside, remember to allow at least 25% extra for wastage. When the ground is snowy, some horses would rather trample and sleep in their hay than eat it, as it might be the only dry spot around!) If he still has trouble maintaining his condition, consider adding a highly digestible fiber source like soaked beet pulp to his daily rations; it can be soaked in warm water to make a satisfying meal that is more nutritionally balanced than a bran mash.

Remember, too, that the incidence of impaction colic goes up in the winter months as many horses don't take in adequate amounts of water. On top of the fact that frozen water troughs and feed buckets may mean that water is often not available, your horse's feed has a lower moisture content in winter (grass, for example, is more than 70% water while hay is less than 10%). Snow, by itself, is *not* enough to take care of a horse's prodigious need for H20, and if you depend on it, your horse will be chronically dehydrated and at risk for impaction.

Make sure your horse always has fresh water available to (consider using stock tank heaters outside and/or heated buckets in your barn). If possible, offer your horse warm water (at a temperature of about 45 to 65 degrees F) at regular intervals. Studies have demonstrated that a horse's water intake in winter increases substantially if he has access to lukewarm water — and if it helps prevent a life-threatening colic, it's well worth the extra effort.

And Finally, a Few Miscellaneous Tips

• When switching from one form of feed to another, do it gradually over a number of days or even weeks. Horses adapt to changes in hay more quickly than they do changes in grain. If you switch from one form of grain to another (for example, if you change from a sweet feed to an extruded ration), expect your horse to take a few days to get used to the difference in format. Start with a small amount and work back up to his usual level.

• Reduce grain by half if your horse is not working — for instance, if an injury forces him to be maintained on stall rest or on a rest day if he is in steady work.

• Remember to feed by weight, not by volume. If you switch from a legume hay to a grass hay, weigh the bales so that you are able to feed an equivalent amount. Likewise, if you switch from oats to a pelleted ration — or even if you switch from one sweet feed brand to another — weigh the amount of the old ration your horse was eating, and then weigh the new ration to find what a comparable volume will be. They will not necessarily be the same level in the coffee can.

• While some horses are just picky eaters, on the whole, a healthy horse usually has a healthy appetite. To tempt a fussy horse, you might have to experiment a bit to discover what he finds most palatable. If your horse consistently leaves some hay and/or grain after he has exercised strenuously, reduce the fiber and bulk in his ration by about 10%. If he still doesn't clean up what he is given, consider that pain induced by his work may be leaving him with no appetite. Try scaling back his workouts to see if that remedies the problem; a veterinary exam also might be in order.

• If a horse cleans up his feed and still appears hungry, first increase the amount of hay or forage he receives by about 10%. Only increase the amount of grain if the horse appears lethargic or is under an increasing workload.

• Ask your local agriculture extension specialist about the levels of selenium in your local soil. Be careful only to use selenium-supplemented feeds if you live in a selenium-deficient area, and never combine a selenium-supplemented feed with another top-dressed supplement containing selenium. The toxicity level of this mineral is unusually low.

• Provide fresh water at all times (except immediately after hard exercise when ingesting large amounts of cold water might cause a horse to colic). It's worth testing your water periodically to ensure it is safe and has no toxic levels of heavy metals or bacteria, particularly if you draw your water from a well.

• Soaking your hay can reduce dust levels significantly. If you have no choice but to feed a dusty hay or if you have a horse with respiratory problems (such as chronic obstructive pulmonary disease, also called 'heaves' or 'broken wind'), wet each flake down thoroughly before you feed it. Wetting hay can also reduce the amount of sugars it contains, which is helpful if you have an insulin-resistant, obesity-prone horse.

• All grains have an inverted calcium:phosphorus ratio — that is, they contain more phosphorus than calcium. Balanced with hay, which has more calcium than phosphorus (especially in the case of legumes), your horse's overall diet usually will end up with a healthy calcium:phosphorus ratio of 1:1, or slightly higher. It's important for the growth and maintenance of good bones, tendons, and ligaments that there is at least as much calcium as phosphorus in the diet; the ideal ratio is 1.2:1 to 1.6:1, but horses can actually tolerate diets with as much as six times calcium as phosphorus without any visible side-effects. If you feed a ration heavy on the concentrates and light on hay and forages, you may need to supplement calcium to achieve a better balance.

• Wheat bran has an extremely inverted calcium:phosphorus ratio — 0.1% calcium to 1.3%, or a 1:13 ratio. As a result, it should never be fed in large quantities on a daily basis, as it is likely to trigger "bran disease" (sometimes called "big head"), a condition in which the horse's system leaches calcium from the bones in order to try to balance the high concentration of phosphorus being consumed. Furthermore, bran has been shown not to have the laxative effect many people credit it with — the loose manure that results after a bran mash is actually the result of a mild digestive upset from a sudden change in feed. A once-a-week bran mash on a cold winter's night, or to tempt the appetite of a convalescing horse, does no harm, but bran should never be fed to young, growing horses; in an adult horse's diet it should make up no more than 10% of the total grain ration.

• Have your hay analyzed each time you get a new batch. Don't assume that bales from the same grower will have the same nutrition from year to year, or even from first cut to second.

• Commercial sweet feeds and pelleted rations may come in two varieties: "least-cost" formulations and "fixed" formulations. In a least-cost formulation, ingredients may be substituted periodically according to the fluctuations of the grain market, in order to keep the price at a constant level. As a result, the nutrition a least-cost formulation delivers may vary quite a bit. A fixed formula, on the other hand, relies on a single recipe that does not change, so its price may fluctuate according to the price of its ingredients. From the point of view of reliable nutrition, a fixed formula feed, while somewhat more expensive, is the better bet.

• When you buy a commercially balanced grain ration and couple it with an appropriate, good-quality hay, extra top-dressing with vitamin/mineral supplements not only is unnecessary but could unbalance the nutrition of the ration. At worst, it might even deliver dangerous quantities of some nutrients; at best, it's a waste of money. Resist the temptation to tinker with what the company's nutritionists have taken so much care to formulate!

• Feed small amounts, often. Horses fed three or even four small grain meals a day have significantly lower incidence of colic and other health problems than those who only get one or two large meals a day.

• No horse will get good value from his feed if his teeth have sharp points or hooks, or if intestinal parasites are battling him for the nutrients he ingests. Have your horse's teeth floated twice-yearly (or more often if he needs it), and de-worm him regularly with a drug such as ivermectin or moxidectin, which kills a wide variety of parasites, including bots. At least once a year, use an anthelmintic which is effective against tapeworms — either a double dose of pyrantel pamoate, or a combined dewormer containing praziquantel.

A Final Thought

A well-known equine nutrition and exercise physiology researcher once remarked to me that, of all the facets of horse management, she thought nutrition was the most poorly understood and most widely mismanaged area of all. If you've gotten this far, congratulations. You're now equipped to go out there and make a difference in how your horses are fed — and to do it from a base of knowledge and common sense.

Major Nutrient Requirements of Horses

Class of Horse (based on mature weight of 500 kg)	Crude Protein (%)	Digestible Energy (DE) in Mcal/kg	Calcium (g)	Phosphorus (g)	Expected Total Feed Eaten (% body-weight/ day)
Nursing foal, 2–4 months (needs above milk)	16	3.3–3.8	0.9	0.6	0.5–0.75
Weanling at 4 months	14.5	2.9	39.1	21.7	2.5–3.5
Weanling at 6 months	14.5	2.9	38.6	21.5	2.5–3.5
Yearling (12 months)	12.5	2.8	37.7	20.9	2.0–3.0
Long yearling (18 months)	12	2.65	37.0	20.6	2.0–2.75
Two-year-old (24 months)	11	2.5	36.7	20.4	2.0–2.5
Mature horse—maintenance (idle)	8	2.0	20.0	14.0	1.5–2.0
Mature horse in light work (eg. pleasure riding)	10	2.45	30.0	18.0	1.5–2.5
Mature horse in moderate work (eg. jumping, cutting, ranch work)	10.5	2.65	35.0	21.0	1.75–2.5
Mature horse in intense work (eg. polo, racing, endurance)	11.5	2.85	40.0	29.0	2.0–3.0
Stallion in breeding season	10	2.4	30.0	18.0	1.5–2.5
Pregnant mare—first four months	8	2.0	20.0	14.0	1.5–2.0
Pregnant mare—7th and 8th months	10	2.25	28.0	20.0	1.5–2.0
Pregnant mare—9th through 11th month	11	2.4	36.0	26.3	1.5–2.0
Nursing mare—first month	13	2.6	59.1	38.3	2.5–3.0
Nursing mare—fourth month	11	2.45	41.7	26.2	2.0–2.5

From Lon D. Lewis's *Feeding and Care of the Horse* (1996), 2nd ed.
Page 411, excerpted from Appendix Table 1 and NRC (2006), 6th ed., Table 16-3,
Daily Nutrient Requirements of Horses (Mature Bodyweight of 500 kg)

Body Condition Scoring System

Condition score	General Condition	Description
1	Very poor	Animal extremely emaciated; no fatty tissues can be felt. Spine bones easily visible, ends feel pointed; tailhead and hip bones prominent, ribs visible and skin furrows between them.
2	Very thin	Animal emaciated, very minimal fat covering. Spine visible but ends feel rounded; tailhead and hip bones obvious. Ribs prominent with slight depressions between them.
3	Thin	Fat buildup halfway on vertical spines, but easily discernible; flat spinal bones not felt. Tailhead prominent, hip bones appear rounded, but visible. Slight flat cover over ribs, but rib outline obvious. Withers prominent but with some fat cover.
4	Moderately thin	Withers not obviously thin; neck carries some fat. Slight ridge along back. Fat felt on tailhead. Faint outline of ribs.
5	Moderate	Neck blends smoothly into body; withers rounded over top. Back is level – spine neither protrudes nor is "buried." Fat around tailhead begins to feel spongy. Ribs not seen but easily felt.
6	Moderately fleshy	Back may have slight inward crease. Fat around tailhead feels soft, as does fat over ribs. Fat layer visible over shoulder.
7	Fleshy	Visible fat deposits on neck and behind shoulder. Firm fat covering over withers. Slight inward crease down back. Individual ribs can still be felt.
8	Fat	Noticeable thickening of neck; area behind shoulder filled in flush with the body. Crease down back quite evident. Tailhead fat, very soft, and flabby. Difficult to feel ribs.
9	Extremely fat	Bulging fat on neck, shoulder, and withers. Obvious deep crease down back. Patchy fat over ribs. Fat along inner hind legs may rub together. Flank filled with flush.

(adapted from Henneke et al. [1983], *Equine Vet Journal*, 371–372)

Amount of Feed Recommended for Growing Horses

Horse	Age (months)	Grain mix (% of Total Diet)	Kg of Grain mix per 100 kg bodyweight/ day	Kg grain mix/day/ month of age for ponies**	Kg grain mix/day/ month of age for horses
Nursing foals	0–4	100	0.5–0.75	0.1	0.45
Weanlings	4–12	70	1.7–2.0	0.25	0.7
Yearlings	12–18	60	1.3–1.7	*	*
Long yearlings	18–24	50	1.0–1.25	*	*
Two-year-olds	24–36	50	1.0–1.25	*	*

* For all ages of horses, feed grain only up to a maximum of 0.9 kg/100 kg of anticipated mature weight per day.
** Ponies: anticipated mature weight of 225 kg (500 lbs) or less.

From Lon Lewis, *Feeding and Care of the Horse* (1996), 2nd ed.
(Page 267, Table 15-3)

Horses' Major Nutrient Needs in Diet Dry Matter as Compared to the Content of Common Feeds

	Digestible Energy Mcal/kg	Protein (%)	Calcium (%)	Phospho-rous (%)
Needed for:				
Maintenance	2.0	8	0.25	0.20
Working horses and breeding stallions	2.5–2.9	10–11	0.3	0.25
Aged horses	2.2	10	0.25	0.25
Composition of:				
Legumes	2.2–2.4	15–20	0.8–2.0	0.15–0.3
Grasses, mature	1.5–2.2	6–10	0.3–0.5	0.15–0.3
Cereal grains	3.3–3.7	9–12	0.02–0.1	0.25–0.35

From Lon Lewis, *Feeding and Care of the Horse* (1996), 2nd ed.
(Page 187, Table 10-1)

Digestive Disorders

W
e are what we eat! This hits home when we examine the broad range of diseases and disorders linked to nutrition. Some of the conditions outlined in this chapter are caused by nutritional imbalances; others have their root cause elsewhere but can be addressed with specialized nutrition.

Developmental Orthopedic Disease

Developmental orthopedic disease (DOD) is a catch-all phrase for related syndromes contributing to poor skeletal development in foals: angular limb deformities, osteochondrosis, osteochondritis dessicans (OCD), contracted tendons, cervical malformations, subchondral bone cysts, club foot, and physitis among them.

Physitis is an inflammation of the growth plates in long bones of a growing foal. (Physitis was formerly known as epiphysitis — but the epiphysis is the site of secondary ossification in a bone while the physis is the actual growth plate.) Osteochondrosis is a process in which cartilages at the ends of long bones are not replaced by bone in the normal manner as a foal grows. The result is thickened, abnormal cartilage, which can separate from the bone and act as an irritant in the joint capsule, causing pain and lameness. Other forms of DOD are variations on the theme of abnormal bone growth in youngsters, and while nutrition doesn't provide all the answers, it does play a role in prevention. Nutritional excesses or imbalances can lead to rapid growth spurts in foals, which have been linked to high incidences of osteochondrosis and physitis — especially in the crucial period when foals are weaned and transition from milk to solid food. Offering a "creep" ration (a highly digestible grain mix designed to support growing foals, and kept out of reach of their moms) can help ease this transition and keep the growth curve smooth and gradual. Diets too high in energy also have been linked to OCD and physitis; prevention can be as simple as reducing the grain portion of the diet, increasing the forage, and offering small meals often rather than large helpings less frequently.

Over the years many different nutrients have taken the blame for DOD, but most have been cleared of the charges as research has continued. Protein, in particular, has been exonerated — meaning that the long-held practice of restricting protein and calories in young horses is counterproductive, as it does nothing to prevent DOD. Instead, it produces reduced growth rates and bone mineralization, even when there is increased mineral support.

Extreme calcium/phosphorus imbalances (such as might be achieved when you feed large quantities of wheat bran) have been implicated in OCD lesions in young horses, and very high doses of calcium can be just as bad because they can interfere with the absorption of other minerals (including zinc, copper, manganese, and iron), all of which play roles in the formation of healthy bone. Copper and zinc (and the proportion of the two in the diet) have gotten attention in the DOD study, as well, but neither has proven to be a magic bullet, though most researchers think foals can benefit from higher levels of these two minerals more than mature horses.

Providing a balanced diet to both pregnant mares and foals, without excessive dietary energy, seems to be the key, along with unrestricted turn-out and exercise. Some research suggests that very high fat diets might not be the best choice for foals because fat levels higher than 10% tend to interfere with the retention of calcium in the body, even when calcium is supplemented. (A fat level of 5% to 6% in the diet does not cause this effect and is more appropriate for youngsters.)

Colic

Few situations strike fear into the hearts of horse owners like colic — the term for any type of abdominal pain in horses. While most cases turn out to be minor, colic is still the No. 1 killer of mature, non-geriatric horses, so the symptoms must always be taken seriously. (Those symptoms range from vague restlessness, loss of appetite, and swinging the head toward the flanks, to severe distress, pawing, sweating, and violent rolling, accompanied by either reduced or increased gut sounds — depending on whether the colic is caused by gas, an impaction, or a torsion of the intestines.)

Recently, researchers have made some significant progress toward identifying specific dietary triggers for colic. All of them stem, at least in part, on the reality that we've removed horses from the wandering, grazing lifestyle for which they're designed. For instance:

• changing the batch or type of hay or grain fed, in the two weeks previous to the colic episode

• feeding hay from round bales (which may harbor more mold, dust, and foreign objects than smaller bales)

• changing the level of physical activity

• decreasing exposure to pasture, again within the two-week period prior to examination

• feeding more than 2.7 kg (six pounds) of grain per day

Why is the equine digestive system so likely to overreact in circumstances like these? The rate of gastric emptying — the speed at which food moves through the stomach and on to the small and then large intestine — seems to be one mitigating factor. When horses graze, they ingest small amounts of fibrous pasture grasses that move slowly and, more or less, continuously through the digestive tract. But when we feed concentrated large meals of grain, there's a decrease in intestinal transit time. Large meals trigger the secretion of profuse saliva and other gastrointestinal juices, which mix with the food and stimulate stomach and intestinal motility (muscular contractions that hustle the food through the GI tract). As a result, there's less time for the stomach and small intestine to break down the grain properly and absorb the nutrients it provides. Boluses of undigested feed may end up being delivered to the large intestine at an accelerated rate, and when they hit the fermentation vat of the cecum, they can start a chain reaction of digestive upset.

Horses in hard training, which often receive generous quantities of grain and a minimum of forage, are especially at risk in this scenario. There's evidence that when carbohydrates (from grain) ferment in the large intestine, a resultant lowering of the pH in the gut occurs, causing hindgut acidosis. As the pH drops, certain beneficial fiber-digesting bacteria die off, leaving the horse with an impaired ability to process hemicellulose. At the same time, endotoxins released by other bacteria as they die damage the gut wall and create excess gas. Spasmodic colic (the "pizza belly" kind) and/or diarrhea frequently result.

Researchers have postulated that large grain meals can have a similar effect in the stomach. While trying to process vast quantities of carbohydrates, the stomach's natural bacteria can produce large amounts of lactic acid, which, in turn, tends to draw water from the plasma space around the stomach, inside the organ. The end result is gastric distension and the risk of a stomach rupture.

Although grain is the major culprit for feed-induced colics, pasture also can be to blame. Most of us are familiar with the dangers of horses gorging on fresh spring grass, but it turns out that certain other growing conditions also can result in high levels of natural sugars, called fructans, in pasture plants. Ingestion of high levels of fructans can create gas colics and/or laminitis, much as a grain overload can. So if your horse isn't accustomed to fresh pasture, it's best to use caution and limit his grazing time, especially in early spring and during Indian summers, when grasses can have a late-fall resurgence in growth. In fact, because plants store sugars during times of stress, fructans can be surprisingly high even in drought-challenged, over-grazed, and recently frosted pastures — so a brown pasture is not necessarily a safe one either!

Another risk factor for pastured horses in some parts of the world is sand colic. In areas where soils are very loose and sandy, horses inadvertently ingest quite a bit of the gritty stuff while they graze and end up with pounds of sand in their intestinal tract, which can cause impactions or even torsions. To prevent sand colic, use a feeder for hay and grain rather than feeding from the ground, and give your horses a supplement containing psyllium husks, which can help whisk the sand through the gut, on a regular basis. (Note: bran mashes are reputed to help shift sand accumulations too, but studies have shown they don't do the job — the bran just floats above the sand instead of moving it.)

Other colic-prevention tips:

• If you're going to do so, change the diet carefully and gradually, introducing new feeds (or larger quantities of feed) in small increments over two to three weeks.

• Consider substituting vegetable oil and fermentable fibers such as beet pulp or soy hulls for part of your horse's grain ration.

• Choose high-quality, digestible hay, rather than stemmy, tough hay that was cut late; the latter will be high in indigestible fiber and may contribute to impaction colic.

• Enhance the digestibility of carbohydrates by feeding grains that have been cooked or heat processed (such as extruded or micronized feeds). This is particularly important for high-performance horses that eat large quantities of carbs each day.

• Provide access to plenty of fresh, clean water to reduce the risk of impaction.

Enteroliths

While we're on the subject of colic, it's worth mentioning enteroliths, curious stony formations that can block your horse's intestinal tract and trigger colic symptoms. They're the equine equivalent of a pearl, forming when a foreign object of some kind ends up in the gastrointestinal tract. That foreign object can be as insignificant as a sliver of wood or a piece of binder twine that didn't get sorted out from the hay. In the rare instance that the body fails to expel the indigestible particle, it tries to protect the gut instead, by encasing the object in layers of mineral deposits, generally composed of magnesium, phosphates, and ammonium (though calcium, iron, aluminum, nickel, and other minerals also are found in some cases). The result is a rocky concretion that may be smooth and spherical, irregular and bumpy, or even polyhedral, depending on the original shape it's trying to cover and the crystalline structure of the minerals involved. Enteroliths can range from pea sized to ones larger than your fist. Small ones are generally passed in the manure (eventually), but larger ones can be responsible for mysterious, recurrent colic and need to be removed surgically before they cause a fatal intestinal rupture.

Enteroliths seem to be common in the southwestern United States, with horses in California suffering a disproportionate number of the intestinal rocks. High magnesium levels found in California water and in the alfalfa hay commonly fed there is the likely culprit. But enteroliths can occur anywhere and can strike any breed or age of horse.

Diagnosing enteroliths is usually done by a combination of radiographs and surgical exploration. The chances of detecting an enterolith by X-ray depend on its location, its size, and the size of the horse (the smaller the stone and the larger the horse, the more likely the enterolith will elude the radiographs). Fortunately, the success rate for removing the stones is upward of 90% — but, of course, this type of abdominal surgery is always risky.

Prevention is the best cure. A few tips will help reduce the chance your horse will develop an enterolith:

• Eliminate, as much as possible, the chance that your horse will ingest a foreign object by removing binder twine from hay and checking his surroundings and paddocks for debris and garbage. Rather than feeding directly on the ground, try a ground-level feed tub or hay feeder.

• Feed grass hay. The 98% of horses with enteroliths have a diet of at least 50% alfalfa hay, which has much higher levels of calcium, magnesium, and protein than grass hay.

• Reduce or eliminate wheat bran from the horse's diet. Bran provides high levels of phosphorus, which may contribute to enterolith formation as well as mineral imbalances in the bones.

• Provide free-choice hay, or at least increase the number of feedings each horse gets per day, to keep the digestive system occupied because when the gut isn't actively moving feed material along its length, it may be providing a favorable environment for enteroliths to incubate and grow.

• Provide daily exercise and avoid prolonged stall confinement. Inactivity also contributes to reduced intestinal movement of feed.

• Bed on straw instead of shavings. Normally we discourage horses from eating their bedding, but where enteroliths are a risk, munching on straw may be a plus — it provides high fiber, bulky feed material throughout the day, and it's low in magnesium, phosphorous, and protein.

Equine Metabolic Syndrome

EMS (a.k.a. insulin resistance; a.k.a. peripheral Cushing's syndrome) is just beginning to be understood in horses. Its typical victim is the easy-keeper horse that tends toward obesity — the one with the cresty neck that looks like a laminitis case waiting to happen. Whether these horses become obese thanks to over-feeding and restricted exercise and then develop EMS, or whether the EMS contributes to the obesity, isn't clear yet, but we do know that abdominal fat stores can exert an influence over hormones, including insulin, the all-important regulator of levels of circulating blood glucose. A horse becomes insulin resistant when the glucose transporters are overworked (by the sheer volume of glucose to process), then fail. When this happens, glucose uptake remains low even when levels of circulating insulin are high. (The equivalent condition in humans is known as Type II diabetes.)

Insulin-resistant horses benefit from a low-carb, high-fiber diet. Anything containing lots of simple sugars should be avoided:

legume hays, grains, molasses, and high-fructan pasture grasses to name a few. These horses usually can derive all the dietary energy they need from grass hay and beet pulp (low or no molasses), or other fiber sources such as soybean hulls, combined with a fat source if they are working hard and having trouble maintaining condition. It's important, however, not to starve EMS horses as that will only make the insulin resistance worse. One study suggests that the fructan level of both grass and legume hays can be reduced by soaking flakes in cold water for 60 minutes or warm water for 30 minutes. There is also some evidence that insulin sensitivity is improved when these horses are kept quite fit.

Laminitis

Laminitis, or founder, is a severe and painful condition of the hooves (generally the front ones, though horses also can founder in the hind feet or in all four). It occurs when some sort of insult or injury triggers vascular constriction that shunts the blood away from the small capillaries and into the larger blood vessels of the leg. When this happens, most of the blood ends up bypassing the feet, and without a steady nutrient supply the cells of the laminae (the vascular tissues on the interior of the hoof wall, which help attach the hoof to the internal structures such as the coffin bone) begin to starve and die. Within hours, the firm, Velcro-like connection between the laminae and the hoof wall begins to disintegrate, and without its stabilizing influence the coffin bone is no longer supported and begins to sink down toward the sole or rotate so it's no longer parallel to the hoof wall. Needless to say, the condition is exquisitely painful for the horse, which ends up rooted to the spot, unwilling to take a single step on his inflamed feet. He may stand with his front feet parked out in front of him or rock back on his heels, trying to relieve the pressure. His feet will likely feel warm to the touch, and a digital pulse (detected in a vessel running down the back of the pastern, near the heels) will be clearly noticeable (in a healthy horse, it's hard to find).

Studies have shown that a laminitis episode may actually begin well before the horse shows any obvious signs. Hours before lameness and pain are evident, the laminae may already be losing shape and function, and once they begin to lose their grip on the hoof capsule, they may trigger a disastrous cascade of events. In the majority of cases, some degree of rotation of the coffin bone is the result, and the greater the differential between its normal position and its rotation, the more severe the laminitis. The pointed tip of the coffin bone, as it rotates, begins to compress the soft vascular "bed" that lines the hoof's inner sole, and that can cause severe damage to the complex maze of nerves and vessels that supply nutrients to the hoof's interior structures and become a major source of continuing pain, long after the initial laminitis attack.

One of the insidious things about laminitis is that the foot may continue to deteriorate long after the episode that first triggered the vascular changes. As tissues continue to die, the coffin bone may end up in a more and more unnatural position, sometimes sinking right through the bottom of the sole over days or weeks.

The causes of laminitis are amazingly complex and under continuing investigation. For all we already know, it's estimated that a good 40% of laminitis cases are still "of unknown origin." However, there are some obvious nutritional triggers, including:

• grain overload, such as might happen when a horse breaks into the feed room and gorges

• consuming pasture high in fructans (see colic, above)

• toxemia (the circulation of toxins, either bacterial, viral, or chemical, in the bloodstream) after a severe injury or insult

Generally speaking, horses and ponies with exceptionally efficient metabolisms — easy-keeper pony breeds, in particular — are most vulnerable to laminitis. These animals benefit from a diet with little or no grain, and restricted access to fresh pasture (either by way of a "starvation paddock" with limited grazing, or a flexible grazing muzzle, which makes them work for every blade). It's also important to keep laminitis-prone horses and ponies from becoming obese.

Gastric Ulcers

Ten years ago gastric ulcers weren't even on our radar. Now, we know that up to 90% of young racehorses, perhaps 60% of performance horses, and even a surprising number of foals, yearlings, and backyard pleasure horses suffer from the distressing symptoms of ulcers in the stomach lining. It's been estimated that virtually all domestic horses will brew an ulcer at some point in their lives.

Gastric ulcers manifest themselves in lost appetite, intermittent diarrhea or bouts of colic, decreased performance, and changes in disposition (usually for the grumpier). Gastroscopy (passing an endoscopic camera into the stomach) reveals the inner damage: nasty, raw lesions on the upper third of the stomach lining. They're caused by stomach acids splashing past their well-protected normal environs to the squamous-lined upper portion of the stomach and eating away at the mucosa. Extensive research has explained why the stomach acids get overactive. When a wild horse wanders and grazes, he's continually putting small amounts of food in his stomach, and that helps keep the acids from splashing around. But when domestic horses aren't fed free-choice, the empty stomach churns with excess acid, and ulceration of the tissues is the painful result.

Exercise is also a factor. Wild horses exert themselves only when necessary for survival, but we expect our domestic steeds to exercise (sometimes strenuously) on demand. Treadmill studies have shown that at any gait faster than a walk, the abdominal muscles tense, forcing stomach acids upward, similar to the way strenuous exercise can trigger gastro-esophageal reflux disease (GERD) — more familiar to most of us as "heartburn" — in human athletes.

As long as we continue to ask our horses to exert themselves on our behalf, gastric ulcers may remain more the rule than the exception. Fortunately, 99% of horses do respond well to omeprazole, a drug borrowed from human medicine. Once a course of omeprazole has been completed, ulcers often can be kept under control by feeding an equine antacid based on calcium carbonate or sodium bicarbonate. Also, dietary approaches can minimize the risk, foremost of which is feeding small meals often or feeding free choice if possible. Avoid feeding gut-aggravating anti-inflammatory drugs such as bute or acidic supplements such as apple cider vinegar, and make sure your horse's calcium intake is adequate but not excessive. Studies in other species have shown that calcium levels influence the secretion of gastrin, a hormone that stimulates the production of gastric juices. Unnecessarily high levels of dietary calcium may result in too much gastrin, which can contribute to ulcers. Finally, be cautious in giving an ulcer-prone horse electrolytes. In one study, endurance horses that receive regular doses of electrolytes (containing sodium, chloride, potassium, calcium, and magnesium, mixed with water) during competition experienced an increase in both the number and severity of gastric lesions, as well as irritated gums.

An interesting side note about ulcers: It is now suspected that they are at the root of most cases of cribbing (a.k.a. windsucking). The vice is addictive, and once learned will continue even after ulcers are treated — but when a horse that previously did not crib suddenly starts the behavior, the habit can sometimes be nipped in the bud by treating him for gastric ulcers.

Moldy Corn Poisoning

Dozens of types of fungi and molds could potentially attack corn, oats, and barley, especially when the grains are packaged at high moisture levels. Not only does mold pose a threat to your horse's respiratory health when he sticks his nose in a bucket of "furry" feed, but some molds also exude poisons called mycotoxins, which are potentially fatal.

Mycotoxins have the potential to cause reproductive, digestive, neurological, and athletic problems in horses. Add to that list paralysis, hypersensitivity, brain lesions, and a gradual deterioration of organ function, which, in turn, can affect respiration, feed efficiency, and growth rates in youngsters. One of the most dangerous things is that most molds that affect grains don't affect the palatability of the feed. Without a change in the taste or smell of the ration, horses are likely to keep eating, the debilitating effects of the mycotoxins increasing with repeated exposure.

Equine leukoencephalomalacia, or ELEM — more commonly known as moldy corn poisoning — is the most common myco-toxin-related syndrome in horses. It is the result of a fungus called *Fusarium moniliforme*, which often invades corn fields the Midwest, especially when crops are stressed by drought or when conditions are very wet at harvest.

Fusarium produces a toxin called fumonisin, which, when consumed in sufficient quantity over at least one to two weeks, causes liver or neurological problems, beginning at least 10 days after exposure or as late as 90 days afterward. Horses show incoordination and a reduced response to stimuli at first, followed by circling or aimless wandering, hyperexcitability, pressing the head against solid objects, blindness, and partial paralysis. Eventually, the affected animals go down and are unable to get up. These symptoms are a result of extensive brain damage (necropsies reveal a rather horrifying liquefying of portions of the cerebral cortex), and horses that exhibit them usually die within 24 to 48 hours. Those that survive often suffer lifelong neurological defects and liver disease.

To minimize the chance that moldy corn will find its way into your horses' feed tubs, you could eliminate corn from the diet completely — but other grains also have some potential to be infected with molds or fungus, so it's difficult to achieve zero risk. Feed mills, well aware of the dangers of toxic molds, go through several steps to ensure their grain is mold free, including rigorous testing of moisture levels in corn. The risk of mold increases when the seed coat of the corn kernel is compromised, so all processed corn — whether it be cracked, flaked, micronized, or ground — is routinely treated with a buffered mold inhibitor. These non-toxic products are usually sprayed on the grain before it is bagged or mixed into a sweet-feed or pellet formulation. (Mold inhibitors are also useful for high-fat and high-molasses feed mixes, often extending their shelf life by several months.)

Many documented cases of ELEM have been linked to the feeding of corn screenings or off-grade or damaged kernels of corn. So using only top-quality corn, processed and examined by a commercial feed mill, improves your chances of getting fumonisin-free corn.

Fumonisin isn't the only toxin to develop in corn — aflatoxin, which is produced by *Aspergillus* mold is another common one. Nor are other grains, such as oats and barley, immune to mold growth. As a general rule, however, poor growing seasons (which tend to produce damaged kernels) and high moisture content are the biggest risk factors, so choosing a feed with naturally low moisture, such as a pelleted ration, may be a wise move in years when the growing season has been particularly tough. Most pelleted feeds have a moisture level of only 12% to 13%, making them resistant to mold as long as they're stored in a cool, dry environment. If you prefer a sweetfeed, you may want to seek one sold in paper bags, which "breathe" and allow moisture to escape. Try to use your feed supply within a couple of weeks, especially in hot, humid weather, and discard any feed that has gotten wet or has been stored for more than six weeks in the summer.

Alsike Clover Poisoning

Generally speaking, clover is a useful addition to any pasture or hay mix. As members of the legume family, clovers, such as alfalfa, supply lots of quality protein, calcium, and other nutrients to horses, and they're tasty, too.

But all clovers are not created equal. White clover, also known as white Dutch or common clover (*Trifolium repens*) and red clover (*Trifolium pratense*) are common and safe additions to many pasture mixes and hayfields, but the closely related Alsike clover (*Trifolium hybridum*) has been linked to two different health problems in horses — one mostly cosmetic, the other potentially fatal. The trouble is that alsike clover is hardier than most other types of clover, so it tends to proliferate in pastures where the soil is poor or the climate is harsh. Owners not familiar with the differences between clover varieties may not recognize alsike for what it is and unwittingly put their horses at risk. And, unfortunately, some feed-and-seed companies, perhaps unaware of the dangers alsike poses to horses, include this clover in their pasture seed mixes and market them for equine use.

The milder of the two problems alsike is photosensitization. Horses that ingest alsike clover in the summer months and are exposed to sunlight may develop red, blistered muzzles and pasterns, especially if they have white markings with pink skin underneath. In some horses the sunburn can be severe, escalating to large, crusty weeping sores with significant swelling. An examination of the mouth of a photosensitive horse usually will reveal ulcers and tiny, pinpoint hemorrhages of the tongue and gums. Fortunately, the symptoms of photosensitization usually go away once the horse stops grazing on alsike pastures or is no longer exposed to sunlight.

Far more serious is a syndrome sometimes called "big liver disease." It has been linked with long-term exposure to alsike clover for close to 70 years, but researchers still don't fully understand what it is about the clover that triggers it — or why some horses develop the syndrome while others grazing the same pasture do not. Big liver disease doesn't tend to appear in outbreaks but in scattered, individual cases, one or two at a time. It's most common in areas where the soil is poor and the climate cool (in other words, areas where alsike clover flourishes). Some symptoms suggest that a mycotoxin (a poison produced by a fungus that grows on the plant) might be responsible, but as mycotoxins usually proliferate in warm, humid conditions, there's dispute over that theory.

A horse with big liver disease exhibits neurological symptoms: sudden, unexplained blindness, pressing the head against objects, unusual paddling of the forelegs. The interior damage is even more alarming. An abnormal proliferation of the bile ducts in the liver results in scar tissue (biliary cirrhosis) that crowds out the liver's normal cells and interferes with the organ's ability to function.

Blood tests can help reveal the liver dysfunction, but a tissue biopsy may be necessary to assess the type and degree of damage. Often, by the time symptoms are noticed, it's too late to save the horse.

Fortunately, alsike is fairly easy to distinguish from red and white clovers — it averages 15 inches to 30 inches in height, with small pink flowers and no white V on the leaves, while the red and white varieties both have leaves marked with the white V and are much shorter (less than 5 inches tall for white clover, 12 inches to 15 inches for red). If you find you have alsike clover in your pasture, remove your horses from that grazing area, plough it up, and replant.

Fescue Toxicosis

Broodmare owners should be aware of the dangers of grazing pregnant mares on pasture with tall fescue. Tall fescue is frequently infected with a fungus called *Acremonimum coenophialum*, which can trigger delayed labor, retained placentas, agalactia (lack of milk production), and abortion in late-term broodmares. The pasture grass, which grows vigorously in the spring and fall, is widespread throughout the United States, though the endophyte infecting it tends to thrive best in hot, humid climes.

Ingesting infected fescue — either as fresh pasture or as hay — poses no threat to mature horses not used for breeding. A few may develop low-grade symptoms such as stiffness and lethargy. Most adult horses, however, can graze pastures even heavily infested with the fescue endophyte and emerge unscathed. But if you have broodmares, fescue toxicosis is a serious matter.

The best treatment for fescue toxicosis is to remove broodmares from all pasture suspected of having tall fescue at least 60 days before they are due to foal.

There are varieties of "guaranteed endophyte free" fescue with which you can seed your pasture, but even then it's worth monitoring the grass closely, as it's difficult to eradicate previously infected varieties. Non-infected fescue tends to be less vigorous than infected fescue, so it often gets pushed out in a pasture after a couple of years.

Ionophore Poisoning

A class of antibiotic drugs called ionophores to which horses are extraordinarily sensitive are commonly added to some beef cattle and poultry feeds. Ionophores aid feed conversion and weight gain in cattle under stressful conditions; the best known is a drug called monensin sodium (known by various trade names such as Rumensin, Lasalocid, and Naracin).

Ordinarily, these drugs would never be found in horse feeds, but if a batch of feed intended for equines were to be contaminated, a dose of monensin of only 1.0 to 3.0 mg per kilogram of body weight would be enough to kill more than 50% of the horses to which they were administered. Death comes after hours of progressive weakness (especially in the hindquarters), incoordination, disorientation, colic, labored breathing, and profuse sweating. In horses that recover from rumensin poisoning, there can be long-standing cardiac degeneration, unthriftiness, and poor performance, with the possibility of delayed cardiac or circulatory failure.

Because ionophores are such a danger to horses, the best place to buy horse feed is a feed mill that doesn't manufacture these medicated feeds. It's also best not to recycle feed bags that may have been used to package medicated cattle feeds. Horse feeds also should be stored separately from cattle rations, preferably in a completely different area of the warehouse or barn. It goes without saying that you should never feed cattle feeds to horses, even if the price differential makes it tempting. They may look similar, but even without the risk of antibiotic contamination, cattle feeds are poorly designed to meet the special nutritional needs of equines.

Equine Polysaccharide Storage Myopathy

This recently identified disorder is common in draft horses and other heavily muscled breeds. It's genetic in origin and manifests itself as a tendency to tie up — that is, become resistant to moving, with severe muscle pain and stiffness and, later, coffee-colored urine that reflects the muscle damage within. In contrast to other forms of "tying up," such as the exertional rhabdomyolysis sometimes suffered by hard-working young racehorses, EPSM horses sometimes exhibit these symptoms without having exercised at all. They may also suffer stringhalt (a strange characteristic snatching up of the hind legs), "shivers" (muscle trembling in the hindquarters), gait abnormalities, muscle wasting in the shoulders and hindquarters, chronic back pain, and episodic colic. At the root of these problems is a defect in the muscle fibers that makes them unable to use carbohydrates as an energy substrate efficiently. As a result, the horse's body, unable to metabolize grain, ends up with abnormal accumulations of glycogen and polysaccharides in the muscles. It's estimated that up to 50% of draft horses are affected. EPSM is also frequently identified (by muscle biopsy) in some warmblood breeds and even in lighter breeds such as Thoroughbreds and Standardbreds.

Though there's no cure for EPSM, a therapeutic high-fat, low-carbohydrate diet for affected horses frequently has a dramatic impact on their health and well being. The diet replaces grain with high levels of vegetable fats — up to 20%–25% — top-dressed on alfalfa pellets or cubes and/or beet pulp. Because it can sometimes be a struggle to get a horse to accept such a greasy ration, several feed companies now have EPSM-friendly complete feeds, which are more palatable. Improvements in attitude and gait are usually seen within two to four months of feeding a low-carb, high-fat diet.

Because EPSM horses on high-fat diets don't receive the benefit of the other nutrients grains provide (primarily trace minerals and vitamin E), it may be beneficial to feed a good-quality vitamin/mineral supplement and some added vitamin E and selenium.

Hyperlipemia

Hyperlipemia is a peculiar condition that can occur in horses but is more commonly found in ponies and in miniature horses and donkeys, often beginning when an obese pony suddenly drops a lot of weight.

In hyperlipemia, the body perceives itself to be starving, so it releases large quantities of stored lipids (fats) into the blood-stream — generally more than the pony can use. This has the unusual effect of shutting down the appetite. A pony suffering from hyperlipemia is feverish, drowsy, or depressed and might suffer muscle twitching, a lack of coordination, colic, diarrhea, and impaired liver and kidney function. He'll tend to refuse all feed, no matter how tempting.

Hyperlipemia can appear rapidly and has a high fatality rate. It is difficult to treat because the only cure is to feed a high-energy, low-fat diet for one to three weeks to a horse with little enthusiasm for food. Enticing the pony with beet pulp or chaff (chopped hay or oat straw) with molasses, laced with fruit juice, apples, or carrots sometimes does the trick. Some veterinarians administer heparin, an anti-coagulant, to help break down the fats already in the bloodstream; giving insulin and/or glucose also has been investigated as a means of keeping the body from releasing more fats into the blood.

We don't yet fully understand what triggers hyperlipemia, but it might be linked to an enzyme called hormone sensitive lipase (HSL), which under some conditions can stimulate too many free fatty acids to be released from adipose tissue and put into circulation. Mares that have recently foaled or are lactating (producing milk) are the highest-risk group. Stress seems to be a factor, which is why sudden, dramatic weight losses should be avoided, as should heavy loads of internal parasites, shipping stress, and other severe changes in lifestyle.

Hyperkalemic Periodic Paralysis (HYPP)

HYPP results from a gene mutation that originated in the influential Quarter Horse stallion, Impressive. It is inherited as a simple dominant gene, and affected horses may have one or two copies of the gene. Those with a single copy often have only mild episodes of involuntary muscle contractions, weakness, difficulty swallowing, and laryngeal paralysis, but those with a double copy of the HYPP gene are much more severely affected and may suffer convulsions and death due to respiratory and/or heart muscle paralysis. At the root of HYPP is a defect in the sodium channels that regulate the passage of sodium and potassium in and out of muscle tissue cells. The result is a leakage of sodium ions into the cells, and potassium ions out of the cells and into the bloodstream (hyperkalemia). This causes repetitive contractions, first visible over the ribcage and flanks, and sometimes spreading to other muscle groups (even the third eyelid). Potassium concentrations in the blood serum may be three to four times normal.

Genetic testing is gradually weeding the HYPP gene out of the Quarter Horse breed (and other breeds that made good use of the Impressive bloodline, such as Paints and Appaloosas). But there remain many heterozygous HYPP horses, which can be managed successfully by keeping stress levels low and feeding a low-potassium diet (below 1% of the total diet). It's a bit of a challenge because potassium is never in short supply in horse feeds, but smart choices can make it possible. Since legume hays contain more potassium than grass hays, HYPP horses should be kept on timothy or Bermuda grass rather than alfalfa, and potassium-rich molasses and soybean meal should also be avoided.

Soaking hay in warm water for about an hour before feeding can help remove some more potassium. Grain digestion stimulates the release of insulin, which may improve the uptake of potassium by muscle cells, so HYPP horses can benefit from a diet with some grain (plain oats, corn, or barley being preferable to sweetfeeds). Beet pulp is another good choice, provided it is the type without added molasses. Needless to say, most commercial electrolytes and mineral supplements should be avoided. Also, commercially available HYPP rations are available, which can help take the guesswork out of feeding an HYPP-positive horse.

Equine Motor Neuron Disease (EMND)

EMND has been reported in several breeds since it was first

described in 1990 but is most prevalent in Quarter Horses and Thoroughbreds. It's characterized by neuromuscular weakness and muscle atrophy, resembling amyotrophic lateral schlerosis (ALS, or Lou Gehrig's Disease) in humans. Affected horses eventually become unsafe to ride though they may survive for several years. EMND affects the lower motor neurons in the ventral spinal cord and the brainstem and develops gradually in mature horses.

Its cause is unknown, but some researchers have suggested it is linked to a chronic deficiency of green forage in the diet, leading to a shortage of anti-oxidants such as vitamin E. As such, it's seen most often in horses kept in stalls, fed a high grain diet, and rarely, if ever, turned out. At present there's no cure, though Vitamin E supplementation combined with other anti-oxidants, as well as DMSO and/or corticosteroids show some promise.

White Muscle Disease

Also called nutritional myopathy, white muscle disease stems from a Vitamin E/selenium deficiency. It's most often seen in foals up to seven months old. Newborns with white muscle disease are weak and have difficulty standing, nursing, and swallowing. They often end up aspirating milk, which leads to pneumonia. In older foals the deficiency manifests as a sudden onset of lethargy, along with a stiff gait. If untreated, it progresses to an inability to rise and death due to heart failure and pulmonary edema, within a few hours. Symptoms of white muscle disease are usually less severe in adult horses, along the lines of a stiff, stilted gait with an awkward head and neck tilt. Muscle soreness, dark urine, and edema in the tissues of the head and neck are part of the picture too.

The name "white muscle disease" stems from the appearance of the muscle tissues on necropsy — they're unusually pale, sometimes with white streaks.

The good news is that white muscle disease can almost always be reversed if caught early, simply by correctly supplementing vitamin E and selenium.

Glossary

Acid Detergent Fiber — A value used to describe a feed's fiber content, ADF is a measure of the cellulose and lignin content.

Aerobic — Occurring in the presence of air. In terms of exercising horses, aerobic metabolism is fueled by oxygen.

Amino Acids — Simple organic compounds, made up of a basic amino group (COOH) and an acidic carboxyl group. The "building blocks" for the growth and repair of the bones, muscles, etc.

Amylase — A digestive enzyme, secreted by the pancreas, which is instrumental in breaking the alpha bonds of carbohydrates to create smaller disaccharide molecules of maltose.

Anaerobic threshold — The point at which the horse can no longer function by aerobic metabolism, occurring at a heart rate of 140 to 150 beats per minute.

Anemia — Below normal count of red blood cells in the blood.

Anti-oxidant — A substance that prevents tissues or objects from being oxidized (combining with oxygen).

Ascorbate or Ascorbic Acid — Vitamin C.

ATP (adenosine triphosphate) — The only source of energy used by muscles and other body tissues. Energy from carbohydrates, fats, or proteins is converted into ATP to allow transfer to the body tissues for uses such as muscle contraction or brain function.

Beta-carotene — A yellow plant pigment, some of which is converted to vitamin A.

Biotin — A B vitamin, thought to be important for the growth of healthy hooves.

Blister beetles — Poisonous beetles that can inhabit bales of alfalfa hay. Cantharidin, the toxic substance in the beetles, produces inflammation and blisters within a few hours of exposure; ingesting the toxin can cause severe poisoning or even death.

Boot stage — The stage at which seed heads first appear in a hay crop.

Bots — The bot fly's larvae, which attach to the stomach's interior lining and may cause colic, inflammation, and perforation of the stomach wall.

Bran — The grain kernel's outer layer, removed in milling.

Bran disease — Enlarged skull bones caused by a dietary phosphorus excess or calcium deficiency, which can result from feeding large quantities of wheat bran.

Calcium:phosphorus ratio — The amount of calcium with respect to the amount of phosphorus in the diet.

Calorie — If spelled with a small "c," the amount of energy needed to raise the temperature of one gram of water one degree Celsius (sometimes called "standard calorie"); if spelled with a capital "C," the amount of energy needed to raise the temperature of one kilogram of water one degree (also called kilocalorie). One kilocalorie = 1,000 standard calories.

Carbohydrates — Compounds made up of carbon, hydrogen, and oxygen whose major nutritional function is to provide energy.

Cecum — Part of the horse's large intestine, the site of the "fermentation vat" where plant fibers are broken down by beneficial gut bacteria.

Cellulose — A carbohydrate that forms the "skeleton" of most plants.

Chaff — Seed hulls, chopped straw, or low-quality hay, added to feed to make a horse eat more slowly. High in fiber and low in energy.

Chelation — A process by which a mineral is bound to an organic molecule such as a carbohydrate or protein.

Chronic obstructive pulmonary disease (COPD) — Also called heaves or broken wind. A chronic respiratory condition.

Cobalamine — Vitamin B12.

Colic — A catch-all term describing abdominal pain in the horse.

Colon — A portion of the large intestine extending from cecum to rectum.

Complete feed — A feed containing all of the horse's nutrient needs, with the exception of water and salt.

Concentrates — A broad description of high-energy, low-fiber (under 18%) feeds. Most often used to describe grains, but includes anything not forage or roughage.

Crimped — Grain pressed between corrugated rollers to crack the kernels and increase its digestibility.

Crude Fiber — An estimate of the total amount of fiber in a feed.

Crude Protein (CP) — A value based on the overall nitrogen content of a feed. To arrive at a CP value, divide the nitrogen content by 0.16.

Dehydrating — Removing all of the moisture from a feed so as to prevent it from spoiling during storage.

Developmental Orthopedic Disease (DOD) — A blanket term for abnormalities in the growth and development of bones and joints in young horses.

Diarrhea — Loose feces, caused by an above-normal amount of moisture. Nutritional causes include inadequate fiber, excess grain, a sudden change in diet, or a deficiency or excess of selenium.

Digestible energy (DE) — A value used to describe the amount of energy in a feed the horse can use.

Dry lot — A fenced area with no grazing.

Dry matter — The portion of a feed that is not moisture. A feed that is 10% moisture is described as 90% dry matter.

Early bloom — The period from which plants first begin to bloom, until one-tenth are in blossom. Used to describe the growth stage of hay fields.

Easy keeper — An animal requiring less feed than others to maintain good condition. The opposite type of horse is called a "hard keeper."

Electrolytes — Minerals lost in sweat and urine, primarily sodium, potassium, and chloride.

Ergot — A fungus *(Claviceps species)* on the seeds of cereal grains such as rye, wheat, and oats, and grasses such as Kentucky bluegrass. It is poisonous if ingested and causes constriction of the arteries and decreasing blood flow to tissues.

Extrusion — The process of forcing a feed through small openings under high pressure. The sudden release of pressure causes the feed to expand like popping corn.

Fats — Triglycerides composed of glycerol (a long chain of carbon atoms) attached to a fatty acid. Fats are necessary in the horse's diet for the absorption of fat-soluble vitamins, for body structure, and for energy.

Fat-soluble vitamins — Vitamins A, D, E, and K, absorbed in the small intestine and can be reserved in the fatty tissues.

Fiber — A carbohydrate composed of simple sugars bound by "beta bonds" that must be broken in the intestinal tract by gut microflora in order for the horse to utilize the energy contained in the feed.

Fixed formulation — A commercial grain mix with a set recipe.

Forage — Plant material, usually grasses (fresh or dried), that make up the basis of the equine diet. Forage may be any feed containing more than 18% crude fiber.

Founder — See laminitis.

Free-choice — Feed or water made available to the horse so that he can consume as much as he chooses.

Gastrointestinal tract — The internal organs responsible for digestion.

Glucagon — A hormone that converts stored glycogen back into glucose and releasing it into the bloodstream.

Glucose — A simple sugar or monosaccharide metabolized for energy.

Glycogen — A storage form of glucose.

Glycolysis — The utilization of glucose and glycogen.

Grain — The seeds of plants, such as corn, oats, barley, wheat, and rice.

Groats — Cereal grain kernels after the hulls have been removed; usually used to describe hull-less oats.

Haylage — Hay or grass cut and placed in plastic to ferment before it dries. Highly nutritious but vulnerable to mold and bacterial growth if the packaging is punctured. Also called "horsehage."

Heartgirth — The circumference of the horse around the barrel, just behind the front legs (roughly where the heart is located). Measured to help calculate a horse's weight.

Heaves — See Chronic Obstructive Pulmonary Disease.

Hemicellulose — A polysaccharide molecule that, along with cellulose, makes up the insoluble fiber of a plant.

Hindgut — The large intestine, including the cecum, ascending colon, small colon, rectum, and anus.

Hulls — Outer protective covering of grains.

Ileum — The terminal section of the small intestine.

Insoluble fiber — Hemicellulose plus cellulose, some of which is digestible with the help of fiber-digesting bacteria.

Insulin — A hormone regulating the amount of glucose in the blood.

IU — International Units, a measure used to describe quantities of vitamins in the diet.

Lactase — A digestive enzyme, produced in the cells of the small intestine, which helps break down lactose (milk sugar) into its component monosaccharides. Present only in young horses.

Lactic acid — Produced as a byproduct when glucose or glycogen is used for energy in the absence of oxygen.

Lactose — Milk sugar, a disaccharide consisting of one molecule of glucose bonded to one molecule of galactose. Present in mare's milk.

Laminitis — An inflammation of the laminae of the horse's foot, causing pressure, pain, and tissue damage, and resulting in separation of the hoof wall from the laminae.

Late bloom — The period when the majority of blossoms begin to dry and fall off the plant. Used in regard to hay fields.

Least-cost formulation — A commercial grain ration that has a set price and might substitute certain ingredients, such as protein supplements, when the price of one increases.

Legumes — Plants that obtain nitrogen through bacteria that live in their root nodules. Includes alfalfa, clovers, birdsfoot trefoil, and peas.

Lignasol — A binder used to help hold pelleted grain particles.

Lignin — A major component of the cell wall of some high-fiber plants, lignin contributes to a plant's rigidity. Also one of the three main components of dietary fiber, considered indigestible to the horse.

Linseed — Also called flax seed. A source of oils and protein.

Lipids — See fats.

Lucerne — Alfalfa.

Lysine — The "first limiting" amino acid, important for growth in young horses. If sufficient lysine is not present in the horse's system, he will be unable to utilize fully all the other amino acids available.

Macrominerals — Minerals needed in relatively large quantities.

Maintenance diet — A diet adequate to maintain a horse's condition when he is at rest in a climate where the temperature does not require additional energy to heat or cool the body.

Maltase — A digestive enzyme that breaks down maltose to its monosaccharide components.

Mcal — Megacalorie, the usual unit used in equine nutrition. Equal to 1,000 kilocalories. See also calorie.

Metabolism — Chemical reactions in the body, including the utilization of nutrients following their absorption from the intestine.

Microflora — A normal, beneficial population of bacteria. In the horse's digestive system, gut microflora assist in digestion.

Microminerals — Minerals needed in minute quantities in the horse's diet.

Micronizing — A cooking process for commercial grain feeds, said to improve starch digestibility.

Minerals — Inorganic (non-carbon-containing) elements required in the diet to facilitate many metabolic functions.

Mycotoxins — Harmful substances produced by molds and fungi, growing on feeds particularly in warm, moist conditions.

Neutral Detergent Fiber (NDF) — A value used to describe a feed's fiber content.

Niacin — A B vitamin that has no numerical designation.

Nutrient — Any feed ingredient necessary for the support of life. Includes carbohydrates, fats, proteins, minerals, fiber, vitamins, and water.

Organic molecule — Any molecule containing carbon.

Oxidation — Combining with oxygen.

Palatability — The desirability of a feed (how much a horse wishes to consume it).

Pantothenic acid — A B vitamin, formerly designated B3.

Pellets — Grains that are ground, bound together, and pushed through small holes at low pressure to make cylindrical shapes.

pH — A measurement of acidity or alkalinity, ranging from 0 to 14. A pH level of 7 is neutrality, below that is acidic (has a high hydrogen ion concentration), and above 7 is alkaline or basic (has a low hydrogen ion activity).

Preservatives — Substances added to feed to decrease the rate of decomposition of the nutrients within.

Protein — Chains of amino acids, which are broken up into their components during the digestive process and used for the growth and repair of tissues.

Protein supplements — High protein ingredients used to supplement the protein content of a mixed grain ration. Common plant sources of protein include soybean meal, cottonseed meal, and linseed meal.

Pyroxidine — Vitamin B6.

Renal — Referring to the kidneys.

Retinol — Vitamin A.

Reverse peristalsis — A muscle contraction reflex that sends food back up to the mouth from the stomach. Horses lack this reflex.

Riboflavin — Vitamin B2.

Roughage — A non-forage feed high in fiber (over 18% crude fiber) and low in digestible energy.

Saccharides — Soluble carbohydrates, e.g. starch, sugars, and glycogen.

Silage — Fermented forage plants.

Simple Sugars — Also called monosaccharides, e.g., fructose, glucose, galactose, and xylose.

Soluble Fiber — Highly digestible fiber from the plant's liquid portions, e.g., resin, sap, pectins, and mucilages.

Solubles — Liquids containing dissolved substances obtained from processing animal or plant materials.

Starch — A carbohydrate composed of many glucose molecules attached with alpha bonds. The bonds are broken by digestive enzymes, releasing the glucose molecules so that they can be absorbed and used by the horse.

Straw — The stems of cereal grains, after the removal of the grain or seeds. Used as bedding and also as a high-fiber, low energy "filler" feed.

Sugar — A soluble carbohydrate made up of monosaccharides.

Supplement — A feed additive used to increase the amount of a specific nutrient or nutrients in the diet.

Sweet feed — A grain mix containing molasses.

Tallow — Fat derived from animal sources.

Textured ration — Used by the feed industry to describe a grain mix, usually a sweet feed.

Thiamin — Vitamin B1.

Total Digestible Nutrients (TDN) — A term used to describe the energy density of a feed.

Trace mineral — A mineral required only in very small amounts.

Vitamins — Organic compounds needed in minute amounts for normal body functions.

Volatile Fatty Acids (VFA) — A chain of carbon atoms attached to a carboxylic acid (COOH) and the major source of dietary energy derived from forages and fiber.

Water-soluble vitamins — The B vitamins and vitamin C, readily excreted by the horse and thus must be replaced regularly.

Index

Photo Credits

CHAPTER 2
Dusty Perrin, 16.

CHAPTER 3
Jamie Donaldson, 26.

CHAPTER 4
CLiX Photography, 33;
Anne M. Eberhardt, 34.

CHAPTER 5
Barbara D. Livingston, 42; Anne M. Eberhardt, 44, 48; Brant Gamma, 45.

CHAPTER 6
Harold Campton, 53;
Anne M. Eberhardt, 54, 57.

CHAPTER 9
CLiX Photography, 101;
Karen Briggs, 102, 105.

CHAPTER 10
Anne M. Eberhardt, 110, 117;
CLiX Photography, 112.

CHAPTER 11
Anne M. Eberhardt, 130, 131.

PHOTO WELL
Kendra Bond; Cheryl Manista;
EquiPix; Karen Briggs;
Anne M. Eberhardt; CLiX.

COVER PHOTO
BARBARA D. LIVINGSTON

About the Author

KAREN BRIGGS, B.SC., is a career horsewoman who began riding at the age of eight and didn't, as her parents had hoped, "grow out of it." As an equine nutritionist and horse feed specialist for United Cooperatives of Ontario, a large feed company, she was responsible for researching, designing, and marketing a new line of premium quality feeds for performance, pleasure, and breeding horses, and for providing common-sense nutritional information and ration balancing to customers across the province of Ontario.

She is also a Canadian Equestrian Federation certified riding instructor, and has managed farms and riding schools in both Canada and Bermuda.

Over the past 25 years Karen has worked at both Standardbred and Thoroughbred racing stables, and competed in disciplines as diverse as Western pleasure, competitive trail, and dressage. She currently concentrates on three-day eventing and provides nutritional advice on a consulting basis. She writes for numerous equine magazines.